Balm in Gilead

Balm in Gilead
Writings of Jeremiah

M. K. HAMMOND

For my dear friend Fred,
Keep the faith !
With warmest regards,
Marie

Resource *Publications*

An imprint of *Wipf and Stock Publishers*
199 West 8th Avenue • Eugene OR 97401

BALM IN GILEAD
Writings of Jeremiah

ISBN 13: 978-1-55635-108-2

Manufactured in the U.S.A.

Cover photograph used by permission of Duke University
The Prophet Jeremiah
South Transept Window
Duke University Chapel
Photographer: Charles M. Register

To Judy Hogan,
teacher & friend

Sometimes I feel discouraged,
and think my work's in vain.
But then the Holy Spirit
revives my soul again.

There is a balm in Gilead
to make the wounded whole;
there is a balm in Gilead
to heal the sin-sick soul.

—African-American spiritual

Contents

Introduction

Jeremiah was a prophet who lived in Jerusalem during the Babylonian invasions, about 600 years before the birth of Christ. In biblical times, a prophet was not primarily one who predicted the future (though some did), but rather one who spoke the word of God. In today's culture such a person might be called a "moral critic" or a "street preacher," depending on the mode of expression.

Prophets, ancient or modern, are sure to offend people, make enemies, and perhaps put their own lives in danger. Jeremiah certainly did antagonize many of his fellow Jews, especially among the hierarchy of princes, priests, and prophets. In his low moments, Jeremiah questioned God and sometimes felt abandoned by him, yet he could not turn away from his calling as prophet of the Lord. Much of what Jeremiah preached twenty-six centuries ago applies equally well in today's turbulent world.

This account of Jeremiah's life is told "in his own words" through letters, sermons, and diary entries. It is based closely on the biblical record, especially on the book of *Jeremiah*, but also on historical books telling about the period and other writings, such as *Psalms* and *Hosea*, with which the prophet would have been familiar. Fictional characters are introduced alongside those mentioned in the Bible in order to fill in details and explain why Jeremiah felt as he did. Unlike the biblical book of *Jeremiah*, this modern retelling unfolds in chronological order, beginning at the disappearance of King Jehoiakim. Earlier events in Jeremiah's life are presented as flashbacks.

Italicized passages in the text are actual quotations from the Bible (Revised Standard Version), identified at the end of the book under the heading "Scripture Citations." These passages point the reader back to the original source, perhaps to reexamine the Bible stories with a new appreciation and understanding.

Looking Back

From Hanniel, son of Elasah, son of Shaphan, to any person who finds and reads these words of the prophet Jeremiah:

Be assured that the documents are as accurate and complete as I could make them. When the scrolls came into my possession, some of them were torn, some faded, and others difficult to read on account of the tiny, irregular script. I have reconstructed, as best I could, the texts which were incomplete.

As to my connection with Jeremiah, it is a long story, a large part of which is revealed in the pages that follow. This much I will say: I knew the prophet quite well when I was a boy, and I was aware that he wrote letters and kept a diary. It happened that we were separated from each other and from our homeland when I was about fifteen years old, but I never forgot about him. As soon as I was able to return to Judah, after some forty years had passed, I began searching for anything Jeremiah had written. I first found, in the city of Mizpah, what remained of his diary, rolled up and stored in jars. A few years later, when the Hebrew captives returned from Babylon, I acquired Jeremiah's letters to his uncle Shallum, carefully preserved and carried back to Jerusalem by a devout old man who had been a friend to Shallum.

The writings span a period of about sixteen years, starting at the beginning of the reign of King Zedekiah, although Jeremiah tells of things that happened much earlier. What he wrote about me and about other members of my family was gratifying to read, but that is not why I have labored to transcribe these writings. Rather, it is because I am convinced that Jeremiah was a true prophet of the Lord.

Second month
1st year Zedekiah

Diary entry:

Such political turmoil I have never seen before in Jerusalem! We still don't know what happened to the king—no one has heard anything of him in five months. He made so many enemies during his lamentable reign (was it really only eleven years?) that it wouldn't surprise me to learn he was assassinated by one of his own people. On the other hand, he was despised by the Babylonians as well. They could easily have executed him during the last siege of Jerusalem. Whether it was the Babylonians or the

Judaeans or his own next of kin matters little to me; the fact is, King Jehoiakim has finally been deprived of the power he abused so shamelessly. I suppose we will always wonder what happened to him, since his body was never found.

For eleven years, the Hebrew people behaved like stupid sheep following their shepherd over the edge of a cliff. This king, this evil shepherd, inspired his people to spread wickedness across the land like dung over the fields. At times, they wallowed so deep in it that I wondered if they could ever again be washed clean. Now I wish I could rejoice that the evil influence of King Jehoiakim is gone, but who knows what will take its place?

His son Jeconiah took for granted that he would be the next king, but the Babylonian generals had other ideas. They saw no reason to grant the Hebrews a king of their own choosing, especially one who shared his father's pro-Egyptian bias. So they sent Prince Jeconiah to Babylon, along with his mother and his advisors, generals, prophets, and priests. (It grieves me that certain members of my own family were deported, including my beloved uncle Shallum.) I was able to say a few words to the prince and his mother just before they left, as the Lord had commanded me to do:

"Take a lowly seat, for your beautiful crown has come down from your head."

For the moment we have Zedekiah as king, appointed by the Babylonians who apparently find him the most acceptable member of the royal family. But the people are confused. Who is their rightful ruler? Is Zedekiah to be regarded as king, or regent, or caretaker until the return of Jeconiah? I wonder, have the Babylonian infidels unwittingly brought about the will of the Lord Yahweh? The prophets in the temple give conflicting testimony—we will soon find out which of them speaks the truth and which spews out lies.

No true prophet of the Lord could have failed to comprehend the evil influence of King Jehoiakim. Yet some who called themselves prophets did just that when they kept proclaiming, "All is well. All is well." How could a man walk through the streets of Jerusalem and not see the cruelty, disease, wretched poverty—the sheer wickedness that was everywhere?

Meanwhile the royal family was hoarding wealth, acquiring power, and building for itself a luxurious palace in which to hide. Did these princes and their priests, who should know the laws of Yahweh, lead the people in the way of righteousness? No, they did not. They behaved worse than anyone else, doing violence to foreign visitors, stealing from poor widows, cheating laborers and abusing slaves for their own gain and pleasure. The princes sought satisfaction wherever they could get it.

"They were well-fed lusty stallions,
each neighing for his neighbor's wife."

While Jehoiakim was king, the Lord told me to say to them:

"What wrong did your fathers find in me that they went far from me,
and went after worthlessness, and became worthless?
They did not say, 'Where is the Lord who brought us up
from the land of Egypt,
who led us in the wilderness, in a land of deserts and pits,
in a land of drought and deep darkness,
in a land that none passes through,
where no man dwells?'
And I brought you into a plentiful land
to enjoy its fruits and its good things.
But when you came in you defiled my land,
and made my heritage an abomination.
The priests did not say, 'Where is the Lord?'
Those who handle the law did not know me;
the rulers transgressed against me;
the prophets prophesied by Baal,
and went after things that do not profit.
My people have committed two evils: they have forsaken me,
the fountain of living waters,
and hewed out cisterns for themselves,
broken cisterns, that can hold no water."

Fourth month
1st year in the reign
of King Zedekiah

Dearest Uncle Shallum,

Your letter arrived yesterday. It is a relief to know that you are treated well by the Babylonians. We have received little news from the exiles, and with my natural inclination to worry, I had feared the worst. I was especially concerned about Orpah; young women who travel great distances are frequently exposed to danger. Your escort of Babylonian soldiers protected you from robbers and marauding gangs, but what about the soldiers themselves? They have been known to use female prisoners (especially the attractive ones) for their own purposes. You are fortunate they behaved well. Now that you are safely arrived, I will rest more easily.

It is regrettable that some of the Hebrew prisoners did not survive the long journey. Your description of their deaths makes me think of the wasting disease, which I have occasionally seen among soldiers and traveling merchants who suffer high fevers and drowsiness like you have described. I will of course inform the families of those who died about the circumstances of their deaths. We heard rumors that young Prince Jeconiah was taken ill. Is this true? Did he recover and enter Babylon with the other captives?

Things are going well enough here. Of course we miss those family members who were carried away, and we have experienced some inconvenience at losing most of our craftsmen. (The Babylonians certainly know how to exploit the resources of a conquered people!) From the latter deprivation, at least, we will soon recover, as the apprentices left behind are quickly honing their skills.

You asked about our new king, appointed lately by our captors. Do you recall King Josiah's third son, who went by the name of Mattaniah? He and I used to play together as boys when my father took me with him to the temple in Jerusalem. The Babylonians have chosen Mattaniah to be the new king in Judah, but they changed his name to Zedekiah; I suppose they think this name change will solidify his change of allegiance. At any rate, he is now known as King Zedekiah.

Some members of the royal family feel that Zedekiah is unsuited for the job, although most of them agree that he will be more successful than his nephew. In three short months, young Prince Jeconiah proved himself to be the pawn of his father's worst advisers. Granted, he was too immature to exert much authority. Few young men at the age of eighteen have confidence in their own sense of right and wrong, much less the self-assurance to impose it on others. Nonetheless, it was a bad beginning for Jeconiah in the office of king. Now he is banished to Babylon, and his uncle Zedekiah will have a chance to prove his mettle.

King Zedekiah is not a bad man. Like his father Josiah, he seems anxious to do what is right in the eyes of the Lord Yahweh. My concern is that he may not be strong enough to resist the pressures which beset him from all sides. Already the war faction is urging him to stockpile weapons and make other preparations in case the opportunity should arise to strike for independence. Fortunately, many cool heads surround the king, and he seems willing to listen to them.

On the other question you raised, I think it unlikely that you will return to Jerusalem very soon. Your captors, the Chaldeans, are a strong people, physically, mentally, and militarily. They have given ample evidence of their strength, as they established supremacy in Babylon and then conquered the rest of the world. The Chaldeans and their king, Nebuchadnezzar, will not relinquish power willingly, and their power depends on keeping our most intelligent and skillful leaders (like yourself) apart from the Hebrew people. You must get settled, Uncle, and make a home for yourself in Babylon. You have lived many years already and must face the possibility that you will not return to the land promised to our forefathers.

It is (as you say) troublesome that you cannot worship and pray in the temple. Yet I am convinced that Yahweh hears you, even from such a great distance. Do you remember, long ago, when we studied together the words of the prophet Hosea?

> *When Israel was a child, I loved him, and out of Egypt I called my son.*
> *It was I who taught Ephraim to walk, I took them up in my arms;*
> *but they did not know that I healed them.*
> *I led them with cords of compassion, with the bands of love,*
> *and I became to them as one who eases the yoke on their jaws,*
> *and I bent down to them and fed them.*

Keep these words close to your heart, Uncle. Yahweh will find you and keep you safe, wherever you are.

I think I have never told you how much those days meant to me, when we studied together in the courtyard of your house in Anathoth. As a young stripling with just a shadow of fuzz on my upper lip, I was full of confidence. Do you remember when I had the audacity to correct the priest on a point of law? You should have silenced me, Uncle (even though I was completely correct in my interpretation). On the other hand, it was amusing to see the old priest's eyes grow big like melons, while he sputtered in disbelief at what he was hearing from an impertinent twelve-year-old. On the other hand, it was disappointing that he did not allow me to continue my studies with him. On the other hand (which adds up to four hands already!), if I had studied with him, I would have spent less time with you, Uncle.

Your wisdom inspired me as we examined the scriptures together. What I will never forget is how you listened and responded to my ideas as if I had been a grown man; that was a gift beyond anything else you could have given me.

I miss you, Uncle.

JEREMIAH

by the hand of Baruch

P.S. I am sending, with the same messenger, a letter to the exiled priests and men of authority and to all the people carried into exile by King Nebuchadnezzar, to tell them the words which the Lord has spoken.

Fourth month
1st year in the reign
of King Zedekiah

Letter to the exiles:

Thus says the Lord of hosts, the God of Israel, to all the exiles whom I have sent into exile from Jerusalem to Babylon: Build houses and live in them; plant gardens and eat their produce. Take wives and have sons and daughters; take wives for your sons, and give your daughters in marriage, that they may bear sons and daughters; multiply there, and do not decrease. But seek the welfare of the city where I have sent you into exile, and pray to the Lord on its behalf, for in its welfare you will find your welfare. For thus says the Lord of hosts, the God of Israel: Do not let your prophets and your diviners who are among you deceive you, and do not listen to the dreams which they dream, for it is a lie which they are prophesying to you in my name; I did not send them, says the Lord.

For thus says the Lord: When seventy years are completed for Babylon, I will visit you, and I will fulfil to you my promise and bring you back to this place. For I know the plans I have for you, says the Lord, plans for welfare and not for evil, to give you a future and a hope. Then you will call upon me and come and pray to me, and I will hear you. You will seek me and find me; when you seek me with all your heart, I will be found by you, says the Lord, and I will restore your fortunes and gather you from all the nations and all the places where I have driven you, says the Lord, and I will bring you back to the place from which I sent you into exile.

Fifth month
1st year Zedekiah

Diary entry:

It is good once again to be able to put my thoughts into words. When Jehoiakim was king, I couldn't keep a diary, for fear that my own words would be used against me. Jehoiakim was a master at finding ways to incriminate those who fell out of favor with him, and my name was always at the top of the list. It is a sad day when a man's private thoughts are not his own, when he exposes himself to danger by confiding in another, when his written words are stolen and used as a license to kill him.

I still do not know whether the plot on my life was instigated by King Jehoiakim. I suspect it was. Nevertheless, knowing that my own brothers participated in the plot was a painful blow. I trusted them; they devised schemes to betray me, promising to cut me down so I could never again prophesy in the name of the Lord. What were they afraid of? Losing their livelihood, I suspect. They were afraid to be expelled from the temple, allowed no more to serve as gatekeepers, after the embarrassment caused by their crazy brother Jeremiah.

Knowing that I cannot trust my own brothers in my father's house has kept me away from Anathoth for seven years. Living in Jerusalem was terribly lonely at first, and still there are moments when I feel isolated. But I have friends. Baruch sticks with me like a true brother. (Heaven forbid he should be like my own brothers!) The family of Shaphan also has embraced me as one of their own and, on occasion, protected me from harm.

Sixth month
1st year Zedekiah

Diary entry:

Reading what I wrote last month in my diary has made me wonder: Are a man's thoughts his own? Does anyone else have a claim on them? It seems to me that a person's thoughts belong to him like nothing else in all creation. A thief may steal a man's mule or his precious stones; a claimant may demand his land or his olive tree; conquering armies might take his wife or cut off his leg, but who can remove a man's thoughts while he is still alive? Who can order a man to think thus-and-so? Others may restrict his actions by force, but who can see his thoughts to tell him what he is allowed to think?

Certainly a man's thoughts belong to no other man, but is it possible they belong to the Lord? Does Yahweh inspire thoughts in the same way he breathes life into us? It must be so, for where else could our thoughts and ideas come from?

A boy imitates his parents and his teachers, but a man has a heart of his own and ideas of his own. If the Lord inspires thoughts, does he sometimes take away the inspiration to think rightly, so that evil influence may come in from a different source?

My questions abound. Does Yahweh give thoughts to an individual or to a nation? About this question, I have an idea that the answer is "both." Ever since my youth, when I accepted the call to be a prophet, I have not refrained from speaking the word of the Lord whenever I hear it, and so the nation hears it too. Are other nations entitled to hear the word of the Lord as well?

My head is spinning with unanswered questions. I must find time to discuss these ideas with Baruch.

Tenth month
1st year in the reign
of King Zedekiah

Dearest Uncle,

Are you well? Have you written any letters since the one you sent when you first arrived in Babylon? Having heard no news lately, I cannot help wondering what has become of you. Please write soon, or send word with a messenger that you and Orpah are still alive.

We are gradually adjusting to the new leadership in Jerusalem. In the ten months since he became king, Zedekiah has made some attempts to reverse the disastrous policies of his brother Jehoiakim. While Jehoiakim did not denounce idol worship, Zedekiah, to his credit, has already spoken against it. Moreover, Zedekiah is promoting observance of Sabbath laws and worship rituals, as well as frequent reading of Torah.

The people seem willing to accept guidance in the worship of Yahweh as long as they are not pushed too hard to abandon their false gods. Why do so many people persist in worshipping idols? I have been pondering this question and have settled on three possible explanations:

First, habit and custom. Their parents did it; their neighbors do it; they have been doing it for years, so it has become ingrained in their daily pattern of life. Wrenching away their charms and amulets would be like cutting away flesh from their bodies.

Second, security. Just in case Yahweh forgets to provide for his people this year, they appeal to other gods for help. Even when things are going well, it is considered prudent to pay lip service to the local gods so they will not be offended.

Third, enjoyment. It is far more pleasurable to visit a cult prostitute and engage in pagan fertility rituals than to study and obey Torah. If people can indulge their lust and ensure good crops at the same time, all in the name of religion, then they will be very religious. But if religion consists in faithfulness to the Lord Yahweh, honesty and fair-dealing with other men, generosity toward the needy, and obedience to laws which restrict their selfish actions, most people will not observe their faith. Human beings rarely pick the difficult path, even though it is the right one.

Yahweh is a jealous God who requires his people to worship him only. The sun and the moon, the rivers and the trees, the earth and its produce are a part of his creation, worthy of our love but not our adoration. It is impossible to worship at one and the same time both the Creator and what he has created; the creation quickly becomes, in human minds, the realm of fertility goddesses.

I regret that the people of Judah have not yet given up their worship of idols (in spite of King Zedekiah's good intentions), and I do not expect them to do so without more painful prodding.

Tell me about religious practices in Babylon. Do the Babylonians worship as many local deities as the Canaanites? Have the exiles thus far been faithful to Yahweh? Are they tempted to follow the local customs?

Please write as soon as you can and relieve my anxiety about your well-being.

JEREMIAH by the hand of Baruch

Twelfth month
1st year Zedekiah

Diary entry:

He appeared again today. Who is this apparition with gleaming white hair, who lurks behind trees and around corners? I begin to think he is a spy for the king, watching to see if he can catch me committing treason; yet it makes no sense. King Zedekiah is not a suspicious man like his brother (who feared even his own mother might stab him in the back). Furthermore, King Zedekiah knows that I hold back nothing from him. In all the years I have known him, ever since we were boys, my thoughts and feelings and doubts have spilled over him like flood waters of the Nile. No, I cannot believe that my shadow-creature is an agent of the king. Nevertheless, I must be cautious.

It has been many months since I have heard a report about the exiles in Babylon. The first and only letter from Uncle Shallum, so full of optimism and good humor, was delivered eight months ago; in the meanwhile, only tiny bits of news have come to my ears. I am worried, not knowing if my dear uncle and his daughter are safe and well. He knows that I worry, so I am certain he has written another letter. Why is the mail delivery so slow? I thought the Chaldeans, with their vaunted efficiency in governmental administration, would have figured out how to run a postal service!

My heart aches for the old man, and I dare not think too much about the horrible dangers to which Orpah is exposed, yet I still believe they have a better chance to survive and serve the Lord in Babylon than they would here in Jerusalem. It makes no sense in my head, but I feel it in my heart.

So far we are relatively comfortable under the occupation. The food supply is adequate, although the Chaldeans who occupy our land take the best wine, oil, and grain for themselves. We expected this (and even worse) of a conquering army, but they have surprised us with their friendliness. The soldiers mingle with our people and try to talk to them. For some reason, I have become a favorite with several of the younger ones; perhaps I remind them of their fathers (or grandfathers).

A thought about my shadow-creature: could the Chaldeans have stationed a spy to watch over me, lest I have too much influence on their young soldiers?

First month
2nd year Zedekiah

Diary entry:

Still no word from Uncle Shallum. It has been a full year since the exiles were taken away from Jerusalem and almost nine months since I received a letter from him.

Shallum and Orpah are dearer to me than any other living members of my family. The long separation and great distance between us have made me realize how close we were; in fact, I still feel they are closer to me than my relations who live in Anathoth. A journey of three hours or a journey of three months—what is the difference if our spirits are united in love and faith?

The love that occurs within a family is a great mystery. My parents had a practical sort of love for each other (and for their children) which was not at all sentimental, but it was real. They willingly served each other and subordinated themselves to each other in a way that did not diminish either one, but made them both stronger and better.

With a greater understanding of love in a family setting, the people of Israel might not have been so easily misled about the expectations of Yahweh. He *never* commanded them to take their sons and daughters to the valley of Hinnom, not when Manasseh was king, nor when Josiah was king, nor when Jehoiakim was king.

Josiah understood the will of Yahweh. He pulled down altars to foreign gods, burned wooden idols, broke down houses of cult prostitutes, and deposed priests who burned incense to Baal and to the sun and the moon. King Josiah forbade the most horrible abomination as well: the sacrifice of children in the valley of Hinnom, who were cast into fire and burned to death to appease the false god Molech.

But the monster Jehoiakim permitted again that detestable practice his father had forbidden. To their everlasting shame, mothers and fathers once again offered their children to imaginary gods. My heart rages when I think of those innocent young children, screaming in pain and fear, as they died a useless death.

With my loved ones so far away, I spend too much time alone. I sometimes feel like my head is a stew pot, foaming and bubbling with a mixture of evil memories. This morning, while it was still dark, I awoke in a cold sweat after a dream in which each of my brothers took a turn at stabbing a young doe, until they had ripped its heart out. My stomach was churning and my heart pounding, so that I was afraid I would be sick if I got up from my bed. As I lay there, my thoughts were racing through the horrible scenes of death I had witnessed in the valley of Hinnom; I remained in this miserable state for several hours, until light dawned.

Fortunately, Baruch came early to my house with good news that diverted my attention and relieved my anxiety. A new baby son has been born into the family of Shaphan, who was secretary to King Josiah. It is the child of his third son Elasah, whose wife gave birth last year to a stillborn child. This one is healthy, says Baruch.

Dear Baruch saw what a sad state I was in when he arrived, so he stayed with me the entire morning and fixed me a bowl of hot porridge. We talked about happier times in our youth and our hopes for better days in the future.

Around noon, we went to see the new baby. The happy household of Shaphan was bustling with activity. Midwives, nurses, and laundry ladies scurried about carrying baskets of clean clothes and herbs and other supplies which are a mystery to us men. Finally we saw the little object of adoration, bundled in so many layers of cloth that only its wrinkled pink face poked out for us to admire. My heart yearned for the child, and then I saw the shadow creature behind him, shaking his head at me. What does it mean? Surely the Babylonians have not stationed a spy to watch over a newborn baby!

A sense of foreboding has again taken hold of me. The people will suffer more than they can imagine for their own sins and for the sins of their leaders.

For the wound of the daughter of my people is my heart wounded,
I mourn, and dismay has taken hold on me.
Is there no balm in Gilead? Is there no physician there?
Why then has the health of the daughter of my people not been restored?
O that my head were waters, and my eyes a fountain of tears,
that I might weep day and night for the slain
of the daughter of my people!

Second month
2nd year Zedekiah

Diary entry:

Finally, a letter has come from my uncle! What a joy it is to know that he is alive and, from the tone of his letter, in good spirits. The old man is allowed adequate leisure time to pursue his studies and his crafts. Meanwhile, Orpah attends one of the ladies in the royal family, a good woman who has taken an interest in the history and customs of the Hebrew captives. The Lord Yahweh is merciful, and I pray that he will keep all the exiles in his tender, loving care.

Baruch penned my response and sent it off this morning. I hope it will be some comfort to Uncle Shallum to learn that Zedekiah is more than a puppet king, and, furthermore, that I am the king's adviser!

Writing to my Uncle Shallum has brought back many memories. I find myself reminiscing not only about the evil days of King Jehoiakim, but also about the hopeful days which preceded them.

When Josiah first became king, before I was born, my parents had high hopes that a new era was dawning for the people of Israel. As a young child, I remember that Mother and Father held the king in high esteem, but they also began to have doubts about some of his policies. One conversation they had at supper when I was about six years old I remember especially well.

My mother asked my father if he thought the king had gone too far. Father said yes, he thought so. "You know I favored most of his reforms," he said, "even the code of worship, which eliminated so much foolishness practiced in the name of religion. But to make Jerusalem the center of all worship? It seems extreme."

Mother responded, "That's not all. We are commanded to make sacrifices in the temple and no place else."

"How presumptuous!" my father answered. "Does the king think Yahweh never leaves his house?"

"I doubt he concerns himself about that. King Josiah only wants to keep tight control of worship so he can be sure the priests do everything according to his standards."

Then Father asked, "What about all those people who are too old and sick or too far away to visit Jerusalem? Does Yahweh not hear them?"

"That question is too hard for me," Mother replied. "Ask the boy."

My father asked me what I thought.

I remember my exact words: "Even if Yahweh is in the temple, he hears to the ends of the earth."

Mother spoke from the pride of her heart, as she was wont to do. "You see, Hilkiah, how Jeremiah is wise beyond his years? Even while he was in the womb, I knew he was called to be a prophet."

My father raised his eyebrows and gave his usual reply, "Yes, dear."

But my mother was right. The Lord had called me to be a prophet, though I was not prepared to accept the call immediately. In the end, of course, Yahweh prevailed. Here is the word which the Lord spoke to me in the days of King Josiah:

> *"Before I formed you in the womb I knew you,*
> > *and before you were born I consecrated you;*
> > *I appointed you a prophet to the nations."*
> *Then I said, "Ah, Lord God! Behold, I do not know how to speak,*
> > *for I am only a youth." But the Lord said to me,*
> *"Do not say, 'I am only a youth';*
> > *for to all to whom I send you you shall go,*
> > *and whatever I command you you shall speak.*
> *Be not afraid of them, for I am with you to deliver you, says the Lord."*
> *Then the Lord put forth his hand and touched my mouth;*
> > *and the Lord said to me,*
> *"Behold, I have put my words in your mouth.*
> *See, I have set you this day over nations and over kingdoms,*
> > *to pluck up and to break down, to destroy and to overthrow,*
> > *to build and to plant."*

Dearest Uncle,

You cannot know how relieved I was to get your letter. A heavy cloak of anxiety has been lifted off my shoulders after such a long time waiting for news. As you can imagine, the people who remain in Jerusalem are somewhat edgy due to the uncertainty of our position; those of us with loved ones far away are especially uneasy. Now that I know you are well, I will try to draw you a picture of our situation here, starting with everyone's favorite topic, the weather.

Yesterday was a stormy day. The thunder and lightning were fearsome, such as I had not seen since my youth. Strong winds and heavy rain continued late into the night, but when the sun rose this morning (and I with it), a glorious calm had descended over the city. The air was clear and fragrant. The leaves of the olive trees shimmered with drops of moisture clinging to them. I wish you could see Jerusalem in such magnificent light as I have seen it this morning.

Our captors continue to treat us as well as we can expect. The people live their daily lives as they always have, except for an occasional glimpse of a Chaldean army unit. The children love to see soldiers; they gather round them like little chicks chirping and pecking. Fortunately, most of the soldiers are patient men, as the children pull on their tassels and chink their armor with stones and shards.

The royal court also continues to function unimpeded for the most part. The Chaldeans have given King Zedekiah a certain amount of authority, which he exercises wisely in day-to-day governance. Although most of us were pleased to learn from your recent letter that Prince Jeconiah has regained his good health, it is also true that the prince is no favorite here in Jerusalem. If he were allowed to return from exile, he would find it difficult to reclaim the throne from his uncle. The people are satisfied with the rule of Zedekiah. They do not wish to be reminded of the evil days when the prince's father, Jehoiakim, ruled the land.

It is amazing to me that I am tolerated in the court (by our own people, you understand) as an adviser to the king. Having been so long out of favor, I was not accustomed to appearing in person before the assembled priests and princes. Now, for the first time in many years, I feel I can speak my opinions in the court without putting my life in danger. To be sure, some of the courtiers regard me as a jester and a source of entertainment when things turn dull. I accept that, as long as I am allowed to speak in the presence of the king. He listens, and I continue to hope that King Zedekiah will be a better ruler than his brother Jehoiakim.

Last evening, Baruch and I began rummaging through an old chest full of scrolls, and what did we find? The sermon I preached by the gate of the temple in the early days of King Jehoiakim, when I was just seventeen years old! It was written out in Baruch's most elegant youthful handwriting. We chuckled in amusement as we glanced over it.

As it turned out, the sermon initiated a difficult time for Baruch and me. I was hauled before the court and accused of treason, spared from the death penalty only because influential friends interceded for me. Later I was beaten and put in the stocks as poor Baruch watched helplessly. He had tried to convince me to soften my rhetoric, but when that failed, he tried (also unsuccessfully) to placate my accusers. Serving as my scribe has caused one frustration after another for the poor man!

Forgive my reminiscing—things are better now.

JEREMIAH
by Baruch

Sermon preached by Jeremiah after King Josiah's death, in the beginning of the reign of his son Jehoiakim:

Hear the word of the Lord, all you men of Judah who enter these gates to worship the Lord. Thus says the Lord of hosts, the God of Israel, Amend your ways and your doings, and I will let you dwell in this place. Do not trust in these deceptive words: "This is the temple of the Lord, the temple of the Lord, the temple of the Lord."

For if you truly amend your ways and your doings, if you truly execute justice one with another, if you do not oppress the alien, the fatherless or the widow, or shed innocent blood in this place, and if you do not go after other gods to your own hurt, then I will let you dwell in this place, in the land that I gave of old to your fathers for ever.

Behold, you trust in deceptive words to no avail. Will you steal, murder, commit adultery, swear falsely, burn incense to Baal, and go after other gods that you have not known, and then come and stand before me in this house, which is called by my name, and say, "We are delivered!"—only to go on doing all these abominations? Has this house, which is called by my name, become a den of robbers in your eyes? Behold, I myself have seen it, says the Lord. Go now to my place that was in Shiloh, where I made my name dwell at first, and see what I did to it for the wickedness of my people Israel. And now, because you have done all these things, says the Lord, and when I spoke to you persistently you did not listen, and when I called you, you did not answer, therefore I will do to the house which is called by my name, and in which you trust, and to the place which I gave to you and to your fathers, as I did to Shiloh. And I will cast you out of my sight, as I cast out all your kinsmen, all the offspring of Ephraim.

> *Third month*
> *2nd year Zedekiah*

Diary entry:

Baruch and I were at first amused when we discovered a manuscript of my first temple sermon. We became more serious, however, when we read the sermon carefully. It was clear to us these many years later that King Josiah's policy on sacrificial worship in the temple (and only in the temple) had had a momentous effect on the people, though surely not the effect he intended.

The stupid Hebrew people came to put all their trust in the temple, and they forgot about Yahweh, whose house it is. The temple became a lucky charm, separate from the Lord and independent of his laws and precepts. With one eye they looked to Yahweh and with the other to Baal; with one hand they offered sacrifices to the Lord and with the other they committed murder; with one foot they walked in the Lord's house, but with the other they ran after foreign gods.

How could people believe that the temple was their salvation? The temple apart from Yahweh is a pile of dead wood and stone. Yet after Josiah died, their new king, Jehoiakim, did nothing to correct the misconception. All he did was to arrest me for speaking the truth. What was the truth? In my sermon I said Yahweh would destroy this temple, just as he destroyed the house of worship in Shiloh.

As the crowd dispersed after I preached that sermon, Baruch warned me that many of the priests and elders were ruthless; they would not hesitate to kill me if I questioned their authority. He begged me to be cautious in what I said and did, and his words proved to be prophetic. Indeed, what I wrote to my uncle about the aftermath of that sermon was not the whole story.

A short time afterwards, the priests and prophets snatched me off the street and said, "You shall die!" A court was assembled in the entryway of the New Gate of the temple, where the royal princes took their seats to hear the case against me. The priests and prophets said to the princes, "This man Jeremiah deserves to die, for he has predicted the downfall of our city."

I was allowed to make my defense. I said the Lord sent me to warn them that this temple and this city will be destroyed if the people do not change their ways and obey God's commands. Then I told them I was at their mercy. They could do with me whatever they wished. But if they killed me, I let them know they would have innocent blood on their hands.

Fortunately, my supporters (especially the sons of Shaphan) spoke up for me. They remembered Micah, who prophesied during the reign of King Hezekiah. Over a hundred years ago, they said, Micah had preached nearly the same message. Did Hezekiah, king of Judah, put Micah to death? No, he did not. Instead, he feared the Lord and begged his favor, and so the Lord relented and did not destroy the city. Thus it happened that King Jehoiakim was persuaded to spare my life on this occasion, and I was released.

Within a few weeks, I made another public appearance at the entry of the Potsherd Gate. I took a potter's earthen flask and smashed it to pieces, to demonstrate how the Lord would smash this people and this city if they continued to forsake him. They would be broken like a pottery jar into a thousand pieces that could never be put back together.

Some of the elders and the senior priests had followed me to the Potsherd Gate, probably because they were curious to hear what I would say this time. Baruch also tagged along. He seemed to understand the danger of the situation better than I did, for he immediately began picking up the pieces of the flask I had broken. The elders gathered around and asked Baruch whose jar it was and if we intended to bring evil and destruction upon Jerusalem by smashing it. Poor Baruch mumbled something about his clumsiness and how he had cut his hand on the sharp edges. Sure enough, he was bleeding over the broken flask while trying to divert their attention from the real troublemaker, namely me.

This time, however, I did not escape punishment. Pashhur, chief officer of the temple, still angry about that sermon I preached weeks earlier, beat me, put me in the public stocks all day and all night, and ordered me to keep away from the temple. It was an inauspicious moment in my public ministry, yet still I managed to get in the last word.

The next day, when Pashhur released me from the stocks, I gave him a scolding he will not soon forget. I told him his name was Terror, and he would see his friends killed in battle, and all his family, including himself, would be taken captive and would die in Babylon. Even now, I can feel the indignation that made me so angry (and foolish) in my younger days.

Baruch scolded me for speaking indiscreetly to a temple official. He practically dragged me away to a safer part of the city and stayed with me to prevent my stirring up more trouble.

Fifth month
2nd year Zedekiah

Diary entry:

Mara. Her name means "bitter," yet she is the sweetest of women. I cannot stop thinking about her.

What do I know about Mara? She is a widow, once married to a merchant of good family who died when she was barely twenty. She has lived since then, for twelve years, with her mother-in-law. Her hair is thick and lustrous with a hint of auburn, and her skin dark and smooth like a glistening olive. What first caught my attention were Mara's eyes, clear and hazel and smiling with intelligence and humor.

Last week I saw her drawing water at the well in the town square. I watched her from a distance, bending her supple body to pull the rope over the side of the well. She laughed with her companions as they filled their jars to the brim and stayed a few minutes after to chat.

As I watched her, someone else watched me. It was my follower, the shadow-figure, standing perfectly still on the opposite side of the square. His white hair gleamed in the brilliant sunshine, else I might not have noticed him at all. He stared at me with a mournful face.

I could not focus my attention on him for long because Mara was moving away from the well, her water jug balanced on one shoulder. She swayed slightly with the weight of it pulling her to one side. I ran alongside to ask if she needed assistance; she shook her head and smiled so sweetly that my heart melted. I turned away so she would not see my lip quiver.

Am I a complete fool to be smitten by such feelings at my age?

Ninth month
2nd year in the reign
of King Zedekiah

My dear Uncle,

I promise I will try not to fret myself so much while waiting for your letters. You are right, of course, in saying that all the worrying does me no good, but you know I have been a worrier since childhood. From now on, I resolve to write you every few months, whether or not I have heard from you. When I receive no letters over a long period, I will assume mail delivery is slower than usual.

Thank you for your commiseration in the matter of the temple sermon and its aftermath. It was a frightening time; had I been old and worn out (as I feel now), I might not have survived the physical and mental demands of life as a convict. During the remainder of Jehoiakim's reign, Baruch frequently implored me to be more discreet and to do my work out of the king's earshot.

Though it is painful to recall, the reign of King Jehoiakim served a useful purpose in my life: it pushed me to begin speaking out in public, even at the risk of embarrassing and injuring myself and my family. Your brother, my dear father, never asked me to keep silent, though I know he suffered humiliation for my sake. My poor mother also was taunted about her son, "weeping Jeremiah," who cried like a mama's boy when his porridge was too hot.

No, it was not the porridge that made me cry but the evil committed by King Jehoiakim and his false prophets, who said only what people wanted to hear for their own ease and comfort. The king and the people paid homage to economic profits, but turned away from the Lord's prophets. Acting out of selfishness and greed, Jehoiakim reversed the good works his father had accomplished and stopped at nothing to preserve his own power and wealth. Sometimes his most faithful friends were crushed underfoot.

Do you remember how my friend Uriah the prophet tried to steer the king away from unwise policies that were alienating his subjects? When the king would not listen to him, Uriah preached instead to the princes and the people, imploring them to refrain from violence, oppression, and bloodshed (some of the king's favorite tactics). But King Jehoiakim, when he heard what Uriah was saying, decided to have him killed. Uriah escaped to Egypt, where he could do the king no harm; nevertheless, Jehoiakim sent his men after Uriah to fetch him back to Jerusalem. After Uriah was dragged into court, King Jehoiakim stripped him naked and scratched red stripes across his chest with the tip of his sword. As the blood was trickling down his body, the king ran the sword through Uriah's belly and watched him bleed to death. In triumph, he commanded that the body be removed to the burial place of the common people.

I wish the king had fallen on his own sword. Such a despicable man deserves an early death and the burial of an ass.

Was it any wonder that I wept while King Jehoiakim oppressed the people and betrayed the faith of his fathers? You were lucky to be living outside of Jerusalem when these abominations occurred. Baruch and I saw horrible things during those years, and we are still haunted by fear that wakes us and deprives us of sleep. There is a kind of violence which is impossible to put out of one's mind.

I am sorry to paint such a gloomy picture; in future letters, I will try to write about happier subjects.

"Weeping JEREMIAH" with Baruch

Tenth month
2nd year Zedekiah

Diary entry:

I find myself walking out of my way to pass by Mara's house. On the way to the temple this morning, I saw her picking vegetables in her garden. We had a brief conversation.

"You are out quite early this morning, madam," said I.

"Yes, it is better to work outside before the sun climbs too high."

"Are you not afraid to work alone when the Chaldean troops are moving about?"

"I have no one to work with me, sir."

"You must find a companion, else I will worry that some harm may come to you."

She laughed. "I know you are a prophet, sir, but in this matter your concern is misplaced." She pointed toward the house. "You see, my mother-in-law watches from the window. She may be old and lame, but her voice is fearsome, better than a watchdog."

I bade her be cautious, all the same. As I proceeded to the temple, my heart beat so loudly in my chest that the other noises of the city went unnoticed. It was nearly noon before I could put Mara out of my mind and attend to the work before me.

Twelfth month
2nd year in the reign
of King Zedekiah

Dear Uncle,

My thoughts continue to dwell on that horrible man Jehoiakim, who did so much damage when he was king. His renovation of the royal palace was a typical display of arrogance. First he took the finest materials without paying for them; then he used forced labor and paid the laborers no wages. The luxurious upper rooms he added were paneled with cedar and painted with vermillion, so that they resembled the holy places of the temple. Was Jehoiakim competing with Yahweh? Did he feel his house should be as splendid as the Lord's?

Jehoiakim had an evil heart. He knew, but pretended not to know, what the Lord expects of kings, and he showed only contempt for the prayer of King Solomon:

> *Give the king thy justice, O God, and thy righteousness to the royal son!*
> *May he judge thy people with righteousness, and thy poor with justice!*
> *For he delivers the needy when he calls,*
>   *the poor and him who has no helper.*
> *From oppression and violence he redeems their life;*
>   *and precious is their blood in his sight.*

Jehoiakim was obsessed by his own greed and lust for power, prompting his fickle attempts to court favor with the Egyptians and anyone else who might help him. He must have believed, even then, that Yahweh's words are powerful because he took the trouble to annihilate the words I had dictated and Baruch had written on a scroll. He was hoping to nullify the prophecy contained in that scroll, which said the temple and the city would be destroyed. (I think the part about the city worried him most, because his own possessions were at stake!) Anyway, he could not suppress the words of the Lord. Baruch had already read the prophecy in the presence of the people and the princes. The words were spoken, they were heard, and they will take effect.

Do you realize it has been almost ten years since that episode with the scroll? It was lucky I was not in court the day it was read, or I might have been roasted alive. King Jehoiakim's heart was like a sealed tomb, impenetrable from the outside and rotten on the inside; he was determined not to listen to the words of Yahweh. Do you recall how (according to the account given us by Jehudi) he took his penknife and sliced off pieces of the scroll as soon as they had been read and tossed them into the fire? I can imagine his cutting off fingers and toes and arms and legs to the same purpose.

It was painful for Baruch to learn that the scroll over which he had labored so many hours was destroyed. He never complained, though, even when I dictated to him the entire scroll again, with a few additional oracles. Baruch is a faithful and dedicated scribe, and more than that, he is a friend.

I never told you, Uncle, about the days Baruch and I were hiding in Jerusalem, because I did not wish to alarm you. You remember, we were warned ahead of time that King Jehoiakim might react violently to the

words of the scroll, especially those parts which foretold the likely consequences of his own evil actions. As predicted, the king flew into a rage,
and, since we were frightened for our lives, we kept out of his way.

Some friends showed us to an abandoned wine cellar, not a bad place
to hide if one is compelled to be shut away for any length of time. (The
aroma from empty casks and spilled wine is not entirely unpleasant!) Our
friends brought us food and water, whatever they could push through the
tiny window without attracting attention. Finding a way to dispose of our
own excreted waste was a greater challenge, of which I will spare you the
details.

We lived like this for several months, ever watchful for an attack by
our enemies. It finally came, without warning. We heard someone prying
open the trap door above the wine cellar, which had been sealed shut.
Baruch and I had made preparations, in case this should happen. We
quickly laid ourselves down in troughs we had dug in one corner of the
room and pulled empty casks over our bodies. We held tightly to handles
we had fastened to the bottom of the casks, so they would be difficult to
move. Then we waited.

After lying still and listening for what seemed like an hour to scraping
and hacking noises, we heard unmistakable sounds of men entering the
cellar. My hands were shaking, and I was glad to have something to clutch
in my tight fists. The intruders' eyes had not yet become accustomed to
the dark, I suppose, (or else they were drunk) because they kept running
into things and knocking them over. One man tried to kick over the cask
to which I was clinging, and he must have hurt his foot, because he cried
out. By then, I was lying in a river of sweat, and I dared not breathe too
loudly. I heard the man hobble away, thank the Lord, and after a few more
minutes, all the men left the cellar.

Baruch was more frightened than I. He had soiled his clothes, poor
man, and even now his face is flushed as he writes this account.

As soon as we could, Baruch and I found another place to hide. After
that, we never stayed in one place more than a few days at a time. We hid
ourselves until, finally, the king found other concerns more pressing than
squashing a couple of pesky aphids.

Back then I had been forbidden to speak in the temple, but later, after Jehoiakim disappeared, I was invited to preach there again. Things are
indeed much better now than they were during Jehoiakim's reign. I hope
all goes well with you and Orpah.

Shalom,

J. with Baruch

Hope

Dear Uncle,

I promised I would send you good news, and I will try to do so in this letter. We continue to muddle along here without any major catastrophes. King Zedekiah has his faults, but he is a thousand times more reasonable and honorable than his brother. We actually discuss issues in the court and listen to opposing points of view before the king makes a decision. Perhaps the king is only indulging in ridicule when he turns to me and asks, "What does Yahweh say about this?" At any rate, I answer him in all seriousness.

But if I am to give you good news, I had better not dwell too long on politics. The grandson of Shaphan has lived past his first birthday. He is fat and happy and much adored by his papa and all his elderly aunts. They dandle him on their knees and speak silly words at him, acting utterly foolish, as otherwise sensible adults will do in the presence of a baby. Why, the other day, I was visiting his grandfather when the little brat wobbled into the room, followed closely by his father, Elasah. When Elasah saw me, he dropped down on his knees beside his son and began making faces. I could not understand what was going on until the toddler imitated his father's scowl and said gleefully, "Jemmy the Poppet! Jemmy the Poppet!" There was much laughter at the child's brilliant imitation of Jeremiah the Prophet, and I must admit that I went along with the joke.

First I dropped down on my hands and knees so I could be on eye level with the child. Then I made a long face, flapped my lips, and babbled in an unknown foreign tongue. The little boy stood with his eyes fixed on me and his mouth wide open. Only when his father started to laugh did little Hanniel know how to react; then he also laughed and laughed.

Did I tell you his name is Hanniel? His presence in Shaphan's household is surely a sign of the grace of the Lord, in accordance with the name chosen for him.

You will be glad to know that I am less anxious now about my own safety. I recently made complaints against the Lord because the people reproach me and persecute me for doing what I am called to do; my words so often go unheeded that I sometimes feel my vocation is futile as well as dangerous. But the Lord answered me and reassured me:

"Gird up your loins; arise, and say to them everything that I command you. Do not be dismayed by them, lest I dismay you before them. And I, behold, I make you this day a fortified city, an iron pillar, and bronze walls, against the whole land, against the kings of Judah, its princes, its priests, and the people of the land. They will fight against you; but they shall not prevail against you, for I am with you, says the Lord, to deliver you."

May the Lord also protect you from harm, dear Uncle.
JEREMIAH
with Baruch

Fourth month
3rd year in the reign
of King Zedekiah

Dear Uncle Shallum,

Your name always reminds me of Shalom, and thinking of you brings peace and a little relief from the prevailing uneasiness of these times. When I tell Baruch we are to write a letter to you, he is plainly affected the same way I am. We soon start talking about the relatively peaceful years of our youth, and our conversation often ends in laughter, and occasionally, in tears.

Most recently we were reminiscing about life in my home village of Anathoth. In a small place like that, people look out for each other and rescue their neighbors when they are in trouble. For a little boy, neighborly concern can seem like an enemy attack. Once I was carrying home a pot of honey from the market. After looking all around to make sure no one was near me, I stuck my finger in the pot and licked off a big dollop of honey. Before I could take my finger out of my mouth, a shrill voice sounded from a nearby rooftop: "I'm going to tell your mother!" I ran home trembling and confessed all to my somewhat bewildered mother, who in the end was more amused than angry. In spite of such occurrences (or perhaps because of them), I felt immensely secure in the village.

When I was small, we rarely left Anathoth. To me, Jerusalem was a distant and mysterious wall on a hill, just barely visible on a clear day. Father told me about earlier times when all the villagers had gone to live in Jerusalem to escape the Assyrian invaders, but that was long before I (or even he) was born. In fact, I never went to the city until after the reforms of King Josiah were strictly enforced. At that time, of course, Father could no longer perform his priestly duties in Anathoth. He was annoyed at having to travel to the temple in Jerusalem every time he wanted to offer sacrifices to the Lord. Yet, for me, it was exciting and wonderful.

I still remember the first time I saw the splendid rooms and furnishings of the temple: cedar paneling up to the rafters; floors overlaid with shining gold; pots and basins of burnished bronze; gold chains; lampstands, cups and firepans of pure gold; cyprus and olivewood carvings of flowers, palm trees, and cherubim overlaid with gold; richly woven blue, purple, and scarlet curtains; and everything infused with the aroma of oil lamps and fragrant incense. It was an absolute wonder!

My father, your brother, was always diligent in his duties to the villagers. He taught them about the notable men who figured into their history. I need not tell you that the great prophet Samuel was brought up in Shiloh under the tutelage of the priest Eli. Eli's descendents were expelled from Shiloh and sent to live in Anathoth, carrying the priestly traditions with them to our village. In fact, they preserved the traditions of both Samuel and Moses, for the ark of the covenant, containing the tablets of Moses, had been kept by the priests in Shiloh. My father always expected good conduct from the people of Anathoth on account of their distinguished lineage.

Most of the people fulfilled his expectations. But I am still haunted by the notion that Father was disappointed in his own sons. Did he ever say anything to you about this? He certainly loved me, as much as any father loves his son, and he never showed annoyance when I made a fool of myself. Yet I accomplished nothing during his lifetime that he could be proud of.

On the other hand, my brothers achieved some rank in the temple hierarchy while conducting themselves with more decorum and circumspection than I ever did. Yet I suspect they also were a disappointment to Father. For one thing, they squabbled among themselves. For another, they attempted to end an embarrassing situation by killing their own brother (namely me). That was understandable, perhaps, but not very nice! I still stay away from them for fear they will do me harm.

So you see, dear Uncle, family relations are not too good just now. I sometimes wonder whether people would be better off living alone rather than trying to coexist in families. It would be helpful if I could talk to you about it in person. But that is not possible.

Shalom to Shallum,

JEREMIAH and Baruch

Seventh month
3rd year in the reign
of King Zedekiah

Dearest Uncle,

Family life is indeed a great blessing. Having visited Shaphan's household often in the last few months, I can more fully understand the benefits of living with others, even at the expense of peace and quiet. Young children are noisy, messy, fretful, and relentless, and thus, by their constant demands for attention, they teach us to overlook trivialities and focus on important things. I have watched Elasah and his wife, Adah, grow ever more mature and dutiful as they care for their son Hanniel.

Two years ago, you remember, Elasah earned my esteem when he was entrusted by the king to carry my first letter to the exiles in Babylon. Shaphan's other sons are good men as well. His middle son Ahikam, though only a youth at the time, stood by my side more than a decade ago, when I was brought before a jury of princes after my first temple sermon. The priests and prophets said I deserved to die because I had prophesied against Jerusalem, but Ahikam defended me courageously. Were it not for him, I might have enjoyed a very short career as a prophet!

The eldest son Gemariah also has taken my side in controversies with the authorities. He urged King Jehoiakim not to burn the scroll I had written when it was read aloud in court. That was a risky request on his part, since I had already fallen out of favor with the king. Moreover, it was Gemariah who warned Baruch and me to stay away from the court that day, lest we be killed.

So you see, Shaphan and his sons and their wives are my best friends in Jerusalem. More important, they are righteous men and women who listen to the Lord and love him with all their hearts and serve him as a devoted wife serves her husband. I wish all of Judah knew the Lord with the intimacy of a faithful wife, but alas, it is not so. Just as marriages go bad when one partner is unfaithful, so the covenant with Yahweh is broken when Israel plays the harlot.

Yet the Lord loves his people and wants only good for them. He gives peace and fulfillment to those who heed his call. As I observe Shaphan's family, from the youngest to the oldest, supporting, consoling, and encouraging one another, I find myself hoping the Lord will call me to be the father of a large family.

All this talk of family has reminded me to ask you about the royal family in exile. Is Jeconiah still in prison? What accusations have been made against him? Has he attempted to incite rebellion among the exiles?

And what about his mother? Was she put in prison too? Tell me if you can what will become of these two bereft souls who once thought their power and wealth were unassailable.

I am forever grateful that you and Orpah are members of my family, and I have many wonderful memories of the times we spent together.

May the Lord protect you,

JEREMIAH (with Baruch)

Eighth month
3rd year Zedekiah

Diary entry:

Mara occupies my thoughts, more than I care to admit. We often meet (not entirely by chance) in the public square near her house. I have unwittingly learned her daily schedule: the usual time she draws water, when she visits the market, where she meets her friends, and many other small details of her life.

Sometimes, when we are going in the same direction, I walk beside her and offer to carry her packages. We talk about a variety of things, and it amazes me what excellent understanding this woman has of the Hebrew faith and of many other topics as well. She has led a difficult and lonely life, full of disappointments. She lost her parents at an early age and her husband before she knew him well, and so she has had much time and occasion to ponder the meaning of life. As frequently happens with those who have suffered, Mara is full of compassion. Her sympathy extends to all living creatures, but most especially to innocent young children and animals, as I observed recently.

We were walking together one day near the city wall when we saw a little boy huddled in a recess of the wall, looking very sad indeed. He was shedding silent tears as he peered down into a bundle he had placed inside his shirt. I would have passed on by, but Mara insisted that we stop and ask what was the matter.

"They hurt my bird," the boy spurted out between sobs.

"Let me have a look," said Mara in the gentlest tone possible. She carefully lifted a grey dove out of the boy's garment, and we saw that its wing was bloody.

"Who did this?" she asked.

"Dogs. There's a pack that roams near the gate." His account came out slowly in bits and pieces, punctuated by sniffles and hiccups. "My mother said to stay away, but I got too close." (sniff) "One of them attacked my bird, even though it was on a string." (hiccup) "I threw stones at the dog to make it go away, but it caught my bird in its teeth and shook it." At this juncture, he was too overcome with emotion to continue the story.

Mara wrapped the bird in a scarf and handed it to me. She coaxed the boy to stand up, dried his tears, and asked him a few questions. She found out where he lived and learned that his parents raised doves for temple sacrifices. They had given him this bird to raise as a pet, since it was deformed and therefore unsuitable for sacrifice.

We soon set out for home, forming a little procession, with Mara and the boy holding hands and leading the way, and me and the bird following close behind. An observer might have assumed we were a family out for an afternoon stroll, and I was happy to play that role; if someone had asked, I would quite willingly (and blissfully) have acknowledged the woman and boy as my own.

My little dream was shattered when we arrived at Mara's house and her mother-in-law peered out the window and screeched at us.

"What have you dragged home now?"

Mara assured her that the boy, the bird, and I would stay only for a few minutes. Then she cleaned the bird's wing and wrapped it in bands of cloth. To acknowledge the boy's sympathy for his wounded pet, she wrapped a bandage around his arm as well. Then we escorted him to his home and left bird and boy in the care of a grateful and solicitous mother.

I walked alongside Mara as she went back to the market place. When I tried to praise her for her kindness to the boy and the bird, she quickly turned the conversation in another direction, deliberating about what vegetables she would need to buy for supper. Clearly Mara feels no great pride in her acts of charity, but regards them as a matter of course.

As we drew close to the market square, I walked slower and slower, until finally, as we passed into a narrow alleyway, I stopped. Mara had walked a few steps ahead of me, but when she perceived that I was no longer at her side, she also stopped and looked around with a quizzical expression. I beckoned for her to come back to me, and when she did, I took her hand in mine. She asked me if something was the matter, but I could not answer. The words froze on my tongue. I looked into her eyes and shook my head, holding her warm hand in mine for a few moments more. Then I let her go. She smiled and wished me well before she turned away and walked off.

My eyes followed her to the end of the alleyway and then caught sight of something else gleaming from a doorway. I was drawn toward the brightness and saw that it was the white-haired, shiny-faced figure I had seen before, stepping out of the doorway and walking briskly out in the road. I followed it, even as it walked faster and faster. Soon I was running through the streets, pursuing this unknown figure, but I could not catch up with it, nor did I lose sight of it. Finally I was so exhausted from the chase that I sank down on a stone stairway to catch my breath. Then the shadow figure also stopped and looked at me, but he was too far away for me to see the expression on his face. Was he mocking me? Was he showing sympathy? It was impossible to tell. I closed my eyes to rest for a few minutes, and when I opened them again he was gone.

A day never passes when I do not think about Mara, and I wonder whether she is becoming an obsession with me. Is this affecting my work? Is it obvious to others that I am distracted?

So far, I think I have executed my duties as the Lord has revealed them to me, with alacrity and diligence. Yet while I am thinking of her, I am not meditating on the commandments of the law; while I am engaged in conversations with her, I am not preaching to the people; when I lie awake imagining our life together, I am not resting for the labors ahead. I pray that the Lord will show me clearly what he expects of me.

Twelfth month
3rd year in the reign
of King Zedekiah

My dear Uncle Shallum,

Baruch thinks I am crazy. The dear man simply does not understand that I see things and hear things which other people do not. But you know it has been this way since I was a child. I hear the Lord speaking in a corner of my house or in a grove of trees, and it surprises me that others do not hear what I hear.

I remember one time when I was thirteen or fourteen I heard the Lord's voice clearly. It was a foggy morning in early spring and my mother had sent me on an errand. Walking through the village, I turned and saw a glorious sight, an orchard of almond trees in full bloom. The Lord asked me what I saw, and (as my voice was just beginning to change) I squawked some reply. Suddenly, the word "watcher" was echoing in my head, over and over again. I understood then what the Lord was saying to me: just as the white almond blossoms watch for spring, so the Lord watches over his word, to accomplish what he has promised.

Later, while my mother was cooking dinner, I had a vision of a boiling cauldron tipped over by invaders from the north, spilling its steaming contents over the land. The Lord again spoke to me, saying disaster would come from the north as a judgment on the people for their wickedness. It was a fearful word, sure to set in motion horrible events, but surprisingly, the Lord told me not to fear for my own safety.

So you see, Baruch makes a good point. By most people's standards, I am crazy. The odd thing is, Baruch still loves me and sticks by me, even when he finds me unbelievable or, more remarkable still, when his own life is in danger. At times he is stupid though; he said something the other day to which I violently objected.

You recall the scroll the priests found when they cleaned out the temple during King Josiah's reign, the scroll containing the words of Moses? Somewhere in the writing, it says that the Lord will raise up a prophet like Moses and put words in his mouth, so he might speak in the Lord's name. When Baruch read that passage, he assumed it was about me! Nonsense! I told him I have nothing in common with Moses: he was a leader while I am a clown; he had help from his brother and sister while my brothers want to kill me; he was respected and I am scorned.

One small thing I have in common with Moses is that I, too, wish our people would remember and understand their history. They quickly forget how their fellow Jews rebelled against Yahweh again and again and each time suffered the consequences. In the wilderness the people worshipped idols when Moses went up on the mountain to meet the Lord, and they paid a high price—three thousand men killed by the sword and others by plague.

The women, too, should beware. Jezebel lied and murdered so her husband could steal the property of another man, and she incited people to serve Baal instead of Yahweh. The prophet Elijah said Jezebel would die in disgrace, and so it happened: She was cast down from the city wall and trampled by horses. Her blood was spattered on the wall and her flesh eaten by dogs. In the end, her remains appeared like dung on a field. Beware, any woman who incites her husband to do evil in the sight of the Lord!

I have tried to be a teacher to the people, but when I tell these stories, they do not take me seriously. I could understand their disdain if I were a pompous youth, but now that my hair has begun to turn grey, they might do me the courtesy of listening. The people actually walk away, sniggering under their breath or uttering oaths against me.

It seems they have forgotten even the beautiful songs of King David. Remember David's poem about the man who loves the law of the Lord? He is like a tree planted by a river that need not fear scorching heat or prolonged drought. He sends his roots to get water, to keep his leaves green and to bear fruit. But the wicked ones who put their trust in men are like shrubs in the desert, becoming as parched as the land and dry as the chaff that is blown away by the wind.

Ever since the scroll of Moses was found and read aloud to the people, there is no excuse for those who pretend ignorance of the Lord's expectations. The words of Yahweh were discovered; I ate them, and they were delightfully sweet in my mouth and in my heart. But to most people they are bitter, or more likely, they remain untasted.

Your old friend Shaphan and his sons send their greetings. That family is a tree that is surely planted by a river. It has good strong roots and branches, and I am grateful for their friendship.

JEREMIAH
with Baruch

Fourth month
4th year Zedekiah

Diary entry:

It worries me that the "hawks," led by the prophet Hananiah, have gained the king's ear. These men counsel rebellion against Nebuchadnezzar, without truly understanding the consequences. They are eager for war, anticipating great glory for themselves but never considering the more likely outcome: another defeat at the hands of the Babylonians, which would only bring further suffering, deprivation, and humiliation on the people of Judah.

Have these hawkish counselors forgotten so soon the horrors of war? I will speak against them in the court when the Lord gives me the right words.

My affection for Mara continues to cause me anxiety. I feel I should watch over her and protect her, yet I am frustrated in this purpose, partly by the demands on my time and partly by Mara's own fearless nature.

She told me last week that a Babylonian soldier had been eyeing her continually in the marketplace. She had no doubt of his lecherous intentions. One day he started to follow her home, so she led him on a long, circuitous chase through the narrow streets of the city, finally arriving back at the marketplace. Then she proceeded to report him to his captain for leaving his post! The next day he was transferred to another part of the city.

It is useless for me to worry about her safety, yet I can't help it. My chief responsibility is to the Lord and to the faithful people of Judah, of whom Mara is certainly one. But, will I ever be more to her than a prophet of the Lord? How can I make myself useful to her so that she sees me as more than just an ordinary acquaintance?

Fifth month
4th year in the reign
of King Zedekiah

Dear Uncle,

Yahweh has once again commanded me to make a fool of myself. This is how it happened:

Some of the priests and prophets have been advising the king to form an alliance with Edom and Moab and certain other nations; they want him to believe such an alliance might drive out the powerful army of Babylon. This is a lie! The Lord Yahweh has spoken to me more than once, saying the Hebrew people must serve the king of Babylon for many years. If we serve him and do not rebel, the king will allow us to live in peace on our own land. Yet these priests and prophets continue to stir up trouble.

So what could I do? The word of the Lord came to me, telling me to take the yoke of an ox and put it around my neck. Can you imagine how ridiculous I looked, entering the court of King Zedekiah? There stood the stately courtiers and the envoys from other nations, dressed in all their finery, looking down their noses and folding their hands meaningfully while their heads bobbed from side to side. All of a sudden, the clown Jeremiah clomps in from the barnyard. Half the courtiers and envoys fell over laughing, while the other half jeered and whistled.

Yet the king opened his ears and let me speak. I told him that Yahweh had created the earth and all the men and animals on the earth. Who are we to argue when Yahweh chooses to give lands and men and animals to Nebuchadnezzar, King of Babylon? If we attempt to break off this yoke, I said, we will be killed by sword, by famine, and by pestilence.

When I stopped speaking for a moment, the hoots and jeers began again, along with braying and certain other vulgar sounds. The king raised his hand for silence.

I was allowed to continue. As Yahweh commanded me, I told the king and the others that the vessels which had been removed from the temple will not be returned in our lifetime. Other vessels, those which had not been removed when Prince Jeconiah and the noblemen of Judah were taken into exile, will also be carried to Babylon. There they will stay until the Lord decides to return them to this place. Furthermore, I said, the yoke on Israel's neck will not be lifted until many years have passed. After

I finished speaking, I left the palace quickly and heard not a few insults on my way out. But that is not the end of the story, Uncle.

I was worshipping in the temple one afternoon with that ridiculous yoke around my neck, when Hananiah, who fancies himself a prophet, approached me. In his booming voice, Hananiah called out for the priests and people to listen while he spoke to me. He said Yahweh had broken the yoke of the king of Babylon. He said the prince and the other exiles, along with all the vessels taken from the temple, would be returned to Judah within two years.

I told the prophet Hananiah I hoped he was right. I said to him, if what he prophesies comes to pass, then he is indeed a prophet sent by Yahweh. But if not, well then, we would find out the truth one way or another. For some reason, my words made Hananiah angry. He broke the wooden yoke right off my neck. He said the Lord would soon break the yoke of King Nebuchadnezzar, not just from the neck of Judah but from all nations.

Uncle, I must admit it was a relief not to be wearing that heavy neckband any longer. Yet the Lord spoke to me again and said that the wooden bars would be replaced by bars of iron. I hope Yahweh does not expect me to carry a heavy iron yoke on these old shoulders!

The word of the Lord came to me later concerning the false prophet Hananiah, that he would die before the end of the year. Hananiah was not happy to hear that!

So you see, Uncle, things are the same here as they have always been: one spectacle after another.

Your foolish nephew JEREMIAH
with Baruch

Seventh month
4th year in the reign
of King Zedekiah

My dear Uncle,

You will soon have the opportunity to meet our august king, Zedekiah, face-to-face! He and his royal entourage are preparing to travel to Babylon to see King Nebuchadnezzar and (I presume) to visit his own subjects in exile.

Several of King Zedekiah's menservants and court officials are going with him, including Seraiah, Baruch's brother. Do you remember Seraiah? He was the daredevil in his family, who would not hesitate to jump off a high wall at the slightest provocation. Baruch was always more cautious, preferring quiet activities of the mind, like reading and discussing fine points of the law. At any rate, Seraiah has been employed for the past six months as royal quartermaster and scribe, so he will be traveling in an official capacity with the king. Baruch, the homebody, is happy to be left behind.

It seems to be a closely guarded secret as to who initiated this royal visit to Babylon. Was it King Zedekiah's idea, or did Nebuchadnezzar summon him? To be sure, the Babylonians are providing an escort of soldiers, cooks, blacksmiths, and guides, but I would expect this courtesy in any case from one king to another.

I suspect the reason for the long journey is somehow connected to recent machinations in Zedekiah's court. It is possible Zedekiah thinks he is under suspicion (as he should be) after his attempted alliances and intrigues with other nations, even though all his plans came to naught. Still, if the Babylonians heard rumors of a plot against them, the king might wish to reestablish himself in their good graces.

I have dictated to Seraiah an oracle concerning Babylon, which he promised to deliver to the leaders of our people in exile. He is trustworthy and will do as he promises; yet in case he should lose the scrolls through misfortune or by deliberate actions of those who wish to silence the word of the Lord, I am sending the same oracle to you by this post.

You remember when they were boys, Baruch and Seraiah competed with each other in school as they learned the art of penmanship, and today a friendly rivalry still persists. The brothers were sitting side-by-side at my desk when I dictated the oracle for Babylon. They glanced occasionally at each other's work as they formed the letters. Seraiah's pen moved quickly and smoothly across the surface of the scroll; he seemed intent on finishing each page first. Baruch's hand was steadier and more deliberate, producing evenly-spaced letters with curls and jots quite beautiful to the eye. I am fortunate indeed to have Baruch as my scribe!

Here is the oracle:

Declare among the nations and proclaim,
  set up a banner and proclaim, conceal it not, and say:
"Babylon is taken, Bel is put to shame, Merodach is dismayed.
Her images are put to shame, her idols are dismayed."
It is the Lord of hosts who made the earth by his power,
  who established the world by his wisdom,
  and by his understanding stretched out the heavens.

When he utters his voice there is a tumult of waters in the heavens,
  and he makes the mist rise from the ends of the earth.
He makes lightnings for the rain,
  and he brings forth the wind from his storehouses.
Every man is stupid and without knowledge;
  every goldsmith is put to shame by his idols;
  for his images are false, and there is no breath in them.
They are worthless, a work of delusion;
  at the time of their punishment they shall perish.
Not like these is he who is the portion of Jacob,
  for he is the one who formed all things,
  and Israel is the tribe of his inheritance;
  the Lord of hosts is his name.

I trust you will take these scrolls to the prophets and priests living in Babylon so they might instruct the people, that they should not be seduced to worship Babylonian images and idols, nor should they forget the Lord God of Israel.

JEREMIAH
by the hand of Baruch

P.S. Remember Hananiah, the false prophet, who said the exiles would return to Jerusalem within two years? He died last week of a sudden fever.

Tenth month
4th year Zedekiah

Diary entry:

Early this morning, as I passed by Mara's house, I heard a strange, muffled sound coming from the direction of the house. I stopped and stared through the lingering shadows and could barely make out a dim figure standing in the doorway. As I looked and listened, it became apparent that whoever was standing there was sobbing and shuddering.

I hesitated to move or make a sound, for fear of frightening the person. Very soon I realized it was Mara, which gave me all the more reason to hesitate. Would she think me a fool for loitering around her house and, worse, despise me for gawking at her in this unhappy state? Perhaps I could escape unseen.

Yet I did not move. As the light gradually dawned on the front of the house, I could see that she was utterly miserable. Finally I called her name softly. She became quiet, peering out into the road to see who was there. I walked slowly toward the house with my hand raised in greeting.

Her face was stained with tears, and she was still shivering and sobbing under her breath. I put my cloak around her shoulders and guided her into the front room, where we sat down.

I asked what was the matter. She told me haltingly that her mother-in-law had been sick and consequently was in a foul mood. Since her only son, Mara's husband, had died, she had no male relations to provide for her; now she berated Mara for having no sons to look after them in their old age.

I told her that it was not too late for her to bear sons and that I was sure someone would love and protect her and take both her and her mother-in-law into his house. Without intending to, I found myself stroking her hair. She was leaning against me, and eventually her breathing became quiet and regular. In fact, she fell asleep. Naturally, I did not wish to wake her, so I remained still for a long time, admiring her beautiful hair under my chin.

It was noon before I arrived at the temple. I fear this woman is becoming a distraction, undermining my work. Will Yahweh help me see what is to be my proper relationship with her?

> *Eleventh month*
> *4th year in the reign*
> *of King Zedekiah*

Dear Uncle,

Thank you for your recent letter. I assume King Zedekiah had not yet arrived when you wrote it, else you would have mentioned him. We, too, are in the midst of the rainy season, although it sounds as if Babylon has had ten times as much rain this year as Jerusalem. From your description of the rushing torrent of the Euphrates River, I can imagine what an overwhelming sight it must be. Has it been possible to continue holding your worship services by the banks of the river?

You asked about the incident when my brothers tried to kill me. It happened many years ago while Jehoiakim was king. I never said much about it at the time because the scandal would have embarrassed my father, as it certainly did later when it became public knowledge.

Here is how it happened: On a cloudy, wet day I had gone out to do an errand. The rain had temporarily ceased, but moisture was still dripping from the trees and the atmosphere was gloomy. I walked beside a swift creek, swollen by three days of rain. Suddenly, from out of nowhere, a bunch of hoodlums jumped on me. It happened very quickly and they were wearing cloth masks to hide their faces, but I am certain that two of them were my brothers. I recognized their eyes.

They worked hastily to tie my hands and feet after they had pulled a gag tightly into my mouth. Lucky for me, they heard someone coming along the path, and they threw me in the creek before the knots were securely tied on my feet. I sank in a deep pool and stayed on the bottom until I thought my chest would burst. Then I floated slowly to the surface, and, fortunately, came up under the shelf of a flat rock where I could catch a breath of air before submerging again. I bobbed up and down like this for what seemed like an hour, all the while wriggling my hands behind my back to loosen the ropes. When I finally got free I looked carefully up and down the banks of the creek for any sign of my attackers, but they were gone. Grabbing some scrubby bushes along the edge, I pulled myself up on the muddy bank and lay exhausted for some minutes. Then I found a hiding place where I could stay for a few days until the opportunity came to say farewell to my mother and father. Soon after that, I went to live in Jerusalem.

We are commanded in the law to redeem a brother or a cousin who becomes poor and sells himself into slavery. Furthermore, we are not allowed to collect interest when we lend money to a brother, nor may we treat him harshly. Yet my own brothers, who grew up in the same house I did, betrayed me. When I saw them next, these brothers of mine who tried to kill me acted like fawning flatterers with honeyed words dripping from their mouths, but I know they would have cut me in two if they had had the chance. I cannot trust them nor believe what they say.

> *Let every one beware of his neighbor, and put no trust in any brother;*
>   *for every brother is a supplanter,*
>   *and every neighbor goes about as a slanderer.*
> *Every one deceives his neighbor, and no one speaks the truth;*
>   *they have taught their tongue to speak lies;*
>   *they commit iniquity and are too weary to repent.*
> *Heaping oppression upon oppression, and deceit upon deceit,*
>   *they refuse to know me, says the Lord.*

These brothers of mine have learned their history lessons too well, following the bad example of Jacob, the supplanter, who lied and cheated to gain advantages over his brother.

Unfortunately, this was not the last attempt on my life. Do you remember the letter I sent to the exiles soon after you were taken to Babylon, the letter saying you would remain there for a long time? That communication inspired such anger in some of your fellow exiles that they wrote back to the priest Zephaniah asking him to silence the madman who wrote it. Zephaniah was sympathetic to me, but some of the other temple officials made a feeble (but unsuccessful!) attempt to have me kidnapped and killed.

The good coming out of all this was that I finally understood that the Lord was calling me to scatter seeds far and wide and not just to the folks at home. If my own brothers would not listen to me, and were in fact hostile to me, what hope was there to get a hearing from the people close to me? In fact I believe I am supposed to preach to all of Judah and to the northern kingdom of Israel (or what is left of it after the Assyrian conquest). Sometimes I think I am called to preach to the nations outside of Israel as well, but that would be an overwhelming assignment.

I hope I have answered all your questions. Try to keep your feet dry amid the rain and floodwaters, and let me know how the people there react to the king's visit.

Shalom,

JEREMIAH with Baruch

First month
5th year Zedekiah

Diary entry:

Mara has again invited me to dine with her and her mother-in-law. She has been exceptionally kind to me since I "rescued her," as she says, "from her deep distress." I suppose she was thinking of the reassurance I gave her that some man would love her and look after her. I wonder if she has any idea who that man might be?

With my whole heart I am gratified to see her laughing again, her beautiful eyes twinkling with amusement and pleasure. I have to admit to some slightly naughty behavior as I try to make her laugh; I have begun telling jokes at the expense of her mother-in-law. But the old woman is growing so deaf, she doesn't even notice.

Last month, when I was at their house, the old woman was complaining about her troubles with tradesmen. I pretended she was talking about Chaldean army soldiers. The conversation went something like this:

"Those men have been taking advantage of me," she said.

I winked at Mara before answering, "They will take advantage of alluring women, you know, especially when far away from home."

"They never give me what I ask for," she grumbled.

"Your asking price may be too high."

"And they demand too much from a poor old woman."

"They are young and lusty."

"My daughter Mara never offers to confront these men for me."

"That's because she is a woman of virtue."

By this time, Mara was struggling to suppress her laughter. She began coughing and left the room, I think to regain her composure. When she returned, she slapped me playfully on the wrist. Then we proceeded to eat our dinner.

At home, I sometimes sit for hours and think about nothing but Mara. I wonder if she feels anything for me. I believe she does. She seeks out my company and talks to me about everything. We laugh, we look into each other's eyes, and we occasionally touch hands. Still, I am afraid to say what is really on my mind: that I would like her to be my wife. We have known each other for three years, but I'm not confident she has any notion of the depth of my feeling for her. I must be patient so as not to hurt my chances by pressing too hard.

And still I am unsure. Is marriage to be part of my lot in life? I care deeply for Mara and would do almost anything to ensure her happiness, yet I cannot bring myself to take any decisive action. I must wait for the word of the Lord; surely he will make clear to me what he intends.

Third month
5th year in the reign
of King Zedekiah

Dear Uncle,

The king and his entourage have returned from Babylon. There is much excitement here among the people, who love to hear tales of foreign lands and smell exotic spices and see trinkets that dazzle their eyes.

Seraiah told me how he delivered the oracle I had dictated to him before the journey. He said you were there when he read aloud the words of the oracle to the people gathered by the river in Babylon. It must have been a dramatic moment when he finished reading, tied a stone to the scroll, and cast it into the middle of the great Euphrates River, to seal forever the word of the Lord regarding Babylon.

I hope the exiles understood that Yahweh is always ready to welcome back his disobedient children, once they have repented. If they forget the Lord and pay homage to worthless idols, they will inevitably lead sinful lives. But if they remember and teach the ways of the Lord to their children and their children's children, he will welcome them back to Israel with open arms.

King Zedekiah has again disappointed me. He returned from Babylon cockier than ever, having presumed that the oracle against Babylon would bring about the hasty demise of Nebuchadnezzar's kingdom. What a fool! When I argued with him that he was misinterpreting the oracle, he put his hands over his ears and shouted at me that I must leave his court immediately. Two guards escorted me roughly out the gate of the palace.

I hope Zedekiah's visit to Babylon does not result in more trouble for the people in Jerusalem. Perhaps he will come to his senses when he has rested from the long journey.

JEREMIAH
with Baruch

Fifth month
5th year in the reign
of King Zedekiah

Dear Uncle,

Do you remember the Rechabites who came to live in Jerusalem six years ago when Nebuchadnezzar's army first approached the city? Their ancestor was Jonadab, son of Rechab, who commanded that his descendants should not drink wine or build houses or plant crops; rather they should live in tents and follow their flocks and herds. For many generations, the Rechabites have obeyed their ancestor Jonadab. Only the fear of Nebuchadnezzar drove them to the city, and even now they live in tents just inside the city walls.

Do you not think, after living for six years in the city, they might have forgotten the commands made to their forefathers? Well, let me tell you, these people are extraordinary; they refuse to forget! I praised them five years ago in the temple and I will praise them again for their faithful obedience to the commands of their ancestor. Listen to what happened last week:

Baruch and I had gone out late one afternoon to buy wine. With large, ponderous jugs pulling heavily on our shoulder joints, we made slow progress homeward. During one of our rest stops, I heard someone call my name. It was the leader of the Rechabites. He remembered me from our meeting in the temple those many years ago. The gentleman invited us into his tent to share the evening meal, and we could not very well refuse his hospitality.

After we sat down, Baruch offered our host and his sons some of our wine to drink with the meal.

"No, thank you, sir. Our father Jonadab commanded that we should drink no wine all our days."

"My daddy Neriah had no such qualms," said Baruch cheerfully. "Truth be told, he liked a little nip with dinner. Come to think of it, Daddy liked a little nip before dinner, too. And after. You won't be offended, will you, if I wash down this fine meal with a cup or two?"

Before our host could answer, Baruch was already filling his cup with wine from one of our jugs. As dinner proceeded, he grew livelier.

"Come now, my good man," he said. "Let me fill your cup with wine."

"No, my friend. Our father Jonadab . . ."

"Jonadab, Bonadab! This is good stuff. We should celebrate the spring rains! And the sunshine! And our friends! Cheers, I say!"

The Rechabite men raised their eyebrows and exchanged glances with one another. They tried to ignore their tippling guest as we continued to eat our supper, but Baruch would not be ignored. After a time, he stood up before us and sputtered:

"You'll want some wine after you shee how good I can dansh. Lishen to the shong my daddy taught me." He wiggled his hips as he sang:

"Dear friend of mine,
This wonderful wine!
I feel so fine
Whenever I drink
The fruit of the vine."

I knew then it was time to take Baruch home to his bed. Fortunately, the Rechabites seemed more amused than offended, but they were glad, I am sure, when the wine and the wine connoisseur were removed from their dwelling.

My dear Uncle, you can see that the descendants of Jonadab son of Rechab have obeyed his command to drink no wine, and they have kept this pledge right up to the present day. The Lord said to the Rechabites in response to their faithfulness: "Because you have kept all the precepts of your father Jonadab, your family will never lack a man to stand before me."

But the people of Israel have not obeyed the commands of Yahweh, though he repeatedly sent his word to them through the prophets, telling them to turn from their evil ways. Because they did not listen, the Lord Yahweh will bring disaster on Jerusalem and all Judah.

Alas, I am very sorry that once again you must listen to my ranting. I had intended for this letter to be light-hearted, to show you that we can still laugh at ourselves. Somehow I always end by complaining against the people of this place. Nevertheless, I hope you have occasions to laugh and enjoy the good things of life, even while you are living in exile in a foreign land.

Love from JEREMIAH and Baruch

Tenth month
5th year Zedekiah

Diary entry:

People call me a prophet, but what does that mean? Moses said a prophet might be a dreamer of dreams or someone who gives a sign. (On that score I guess I qualify, since I am able to see and interpret signs.) The test of a real prophet, he said, comes when the prophet speaks in the name of the Lord: if the word does not prove to be true, then the prophet has spoken presumptuously and need not be feared. On this point, I must postpone judgment about myself, since the words I preach day after day have not yet taken effect; the people have not repented of their sins, nor have they been punished for their wickedness.

In fact, a prophet's life is full of ambiguities. He tries to listen with open ears for any communication or revelation from the Lord, but how can he be sure it is actually the word of the Lord? Does fulfillment of prophecy always come immediately, or might it wait until after the prophet dies? Is he (or anyone else) able to recognize fulfillment when it happens?

What I know for certain is that if a prophet tells the people to go after other gods and serve them, then he is no prophet of the Lord, and he deserves to be put to death. True prophets do not break the commandments of Moses or steal words from other prophets, nor do they speak their own ideas and attribute them to the Lord. A prophet must be first and foremost a mouthpiece of the Lord. He tells what he has heard, even at the risk of sounding like a fool. In fact, he must be willing to risk his life and reputation when he speaks the word of the Lord.

The prophet Hosea did all this and more. He incorporated what he heard into his life, marrying a harlot, conceiving unfaithful children, pleading with them to return, and then forgiving them, just as the Lord has done for his people many times over. Hosea trusted in the Lord with all his heart, and perhaps that is the mark of a true prophet. Do I possess that level of trust? Only the Lord knows.

Even if I am not a true prophet, I can quote Hosea, who was. At the next opportunity, I will say to the people:

> *Sow for yourselves righteousness, reap the fruit of steadfast love;*
> *break up your fallow ground, for it is the time to seek the Lord,*
> *that he may come and rain salvation upon you.*

Rejection

Dearest Uncle,

Your most recent letter has made me glad indeed. It is a wonderful thing to know that the people of Israel can remain faithful to Yahweh in a distant land. According to your reports (and others), the Jews in Babylon live as though they understand the words of the psalmist:

Our God is in the heavens; he does whatever he pleases.
Their idols are silver and gold, the work of men's hands.
They have mouths, but do not speak; eyes, but do not see.
They have ears, but do not hear; noses, but do not smell.
They have hands, but do not feel; feet, but do not walk;
and they do not make a sound in their throat.
Those who make them are like them; so are all who trust in them.

You say the young men have refused to bow down to Babylonian idols, even upon threat of death? I have seen no such constancy in Judah for many years. The refusal by your fellow exiles to eat unclean foods is another sign that they are closer to Yahweh than those in Jerusalem who stand beside the temple gates.

The Lord showed me a vision: I saw two baskets of figs by the entrance of the temple, one containing good ripe figs and the other containing rotten figs, not fit to eat. The Lord said to me that the people he sent away to Babylon are like the good figs; he will bring them back and plant them and teach everyone to know who he is. Then they will love him with all their hearts.

But the remnant of Israel who stayed in Jerusalem are like the bad figs; they shall be driven from this land by invasions and hunger and disease, and wherever they go they will be despised.

How do you like that, Uncle? Even my lunch inspires a vision! It gives me a new appreciation for fruits and vegetables!

We are the Lord's chosen people, as you often told me, Uncle, but for what are we chosen? The people of Israel are not favored with great wealth or power over other nations. It cannot be said that Yahweh has given us a life of ease and contentment. What then? Are we chosen to suffer? Chosen to be aware of our own sin and misery? Chosen to know that we are punished by Yahweh?

Strangely enough, Uncle, I think we are chosen for all these purposes. Only by awareness of our own shortcomings can we begin to comprehend the majesty of the Lord Yahweh. Then we can know that he is worthy to be loved with our whole heart and soul and might. We might even come to understand how all families and nations of the earth shall be blessed through the faithfulness of Abraham.

It is sad when innocent people suffer for the sins of a few as is happening today in Jerusalem; yet by their acquiescence, the people all become participants in evildoing. A few bad figs make the entire basket turn rotten.

On the other hand, it seems that a few righteous leaders among the exiles have inspired the whole community to turn toward Yahweh. This may sound crazy to you, but I think the insecurity of the exiles has made them secure! You have been deported from your land, deprived of your neighbors, your temple and your daily rituals, and have found something better. To trust in Yahweh and turn to him with your whole heart is a much greater blessing than any plot of earth or secure environment.

What do you think about this, Uncle? Write soon and let me know.

Your devoted nephew,

JEREMIAH, with Baruch

Second month
6th year Zedekiah

Diary entry:

Mara sent a message to me yesterday, saying she desired to talk to me about something of great consequence. Naturally I was ready immediately to dash to her house, but I managed to restrain myself until the appointed time. While I waited, my heart was full, imagining that she knew my feelings for her and that she perhaps felt something for me. Today my face warms when I think of it, whether from affection or from embarrassment, I am not certain.

When I arrived, Mara took my hand and led me to the seat of honor. She handed me a bowl of hot broth, sat down beside me, and waited patiently until I had finished drinking. Then she told me her dilemma: Two men had made her offers of marriage, and she did not know which to accept. This took me by surprise. I could not speak. Thoughts raced through my head and memories from the last four years came clear; all the regard and affection Mara had shown for me were simply that of a daughter for her father, or more accurately, a pupil for her teacher.

She must have thought I was in a trance, preparing to make a prophetic utterance. Instead, I stammered foolishly, and now I can recall absolutely nothing of the "advice" I gave her. Whatever I said cannot have been much help.

Last night my head exploded with dreams. I woke up more than once as a consequence of my own twitching and turning. Most of the dreams made no sense and I soon forgot them, but one I remember in vivid detail:

My pursuer, the shadow figure, stood with grim face and upraised sword in the middle of the market square. All around him lay twisted bodies of young women and children, even newborn babies, piled atop their husbands and fathers. Some of the men underneath were alive, moving and groaning, but the women and children were all dead.

Old men and women stood around the edge of the square staring at the scene of carnage. They carried out none of the usual rituals of mourning: weeping, wailing, tearing their clothes, or dropping dust on their heads. Furthermore, they made no move to comfort one another. They were standing completely still, as if they had been forbidden to mourn in any way for their loved ones. I awoke from this dream soaked with sweat.

Dare I hold out any hope for domestic happiness? Will I ever find a wife to cling to or see little children gathered about my feet? It begins to look like Yahweh has other intentions, and that I will die a lonely old man.

Third month
6th year Zedekiah

Diary entry:

The last three days I have spent in prayer and fasting. I am sunk into a pit of despair as I beseech the Lord to forgive the wicked foolishness of his people Israel. My heart is angry and grieved that they pay so little attention to the words of Yahweh.

As for the leaders, the king and the princes are again plotting a revolt against Nebuchadnezzar. They are talking of withholding the monthly tribute from him in order to preserve their own opulent and obscene way of life. These pig-rulers are not willing to do without delicate foods and gold jewelry, painted harlots and young slave maidens, even when the lives of the people are at stake.

Meanwhile the people themselves, for want of direction and good example, ignore the law and flaunt their wicked behavior. How many Hebrew men I have seen entering the dens of cult prostitutes! How much idol worship and theft and flagrant adultery I have witnessed! Even murder is committed in Jerusalem while the royal princes dance and sing.

The consequences of all these unrighteous actions are unmistakable. The people do not trust each other and dare not expose their backs to their own brothers. Aged widows, for want of attention, die of hunger and thirst. Diseases rack the bodies of young men who satisfy their lust on every street corner. Indications of moral filth are everywhere.

Yet the people choose to ignore the signs and live their lives in stupid heedlessness. I make myself into a living message for them, pleading, crawling, weeping, pounding my chest, all to no avail. They refuse to give up their self-centered attitude, and they refuse to see how their selfishness undermines the community.

The king is no help. He is a coward who will not stand up for the word of the Lord. His positions change at the slightest hint of opposition, like grains of sand in a whirlwind, blown every which way. When the priests of Baal set their gold-plated images before him, he listens to their counsel. They tell him, through sorcery and divination, to ignore the commandments of Yahweh and to rebel against the powerful governments established by the Lord. Better to heed the local gods who have long given succor to those who dwell here, they say.

The king has a mind acute enough to understand what is happening and to know what action is called for, but he lacks the backbone to do it. He is afraid to offend whatever gods might be lurking in the neighborhood. My pleading on behalf of the one Lord who deserves our obedience has no effect—now I can only pray that the Lord will give King Zedekiah the courage to do what is right before we are all destroyed.

This fasting has cleared my head (though my heart remains clouded). On the personal matter before me, I can see plainly that it is my duty to do what Mara asks of me (though it wounds me through and through). I have resolved to meet the two suitors to find out what sort of men they are. Then I trust Yahweh will guide me to do the best I can for this woman.

Fifth month
6th year Zedekiah

Diary entry:

I have been to see Mara. It pained me greatly to tell her what I had found out about her suitors. The one called Zaccai is a rich farmer who owns fifty head of cattle and twice as many sheep, which he keeps in pastures on the south side of the city. He has two daughters living in his house, whose mother died while giving birth to the younger. There is some question about his character, rumors that he may not be an honest man; it is reported that he swindled his elder brother to acquire his land. I did not trouble Mara with this information, since the rumors may be false. I will try to find out more.

The other man, Iddo, works hard at his leather-goods shop and seems friendly enough. His business is always bustling with customers. Yet, his equipment is primitive, he employs no apprentices, and he lives in a tiny room behind the shop. How he expects to keep a wife and children in such accommodations I can't imagine. Mara is obviously very fond of him, I can see that. But nevertheless I am uneasy recommending that she marry him—or the other man, for that matter.

I can see that my new job as marriage broker is not going to be an easy one. I fear I am comparing Mara's suitors to myself, knowing that I could look after her and protect her better than either one of them.

Yet what woman would want to be married to a prophet of the Lord? Gomer the daughter of Diblaim married the prophet Hosea, and when she bore him children, Hosea gave them outlandish names to describe the fate of Israel. Their oldest child was named Jezreel, for the valley where Israel's bow would be broken, and the other children were called "Not Pitied" and "Not My People," because the Lord could no longer acknowledge the kingdom of Jeroboam as his people.

Would I inflict a similar shame on Mara, were she to become my wife and bear my children? I hope not, but if the Lord commanded me, could I disobey?

Sixth month
6th year Zedekiah

Diary entry:

Now I *know* this Zaccai fellow is a scoundrel. I went to see him today and his behavior was even worse than I expected. He looked at me suspiciously from the moment I entered his house. We sat down in the gloom of a small, dark room with no windows and said few words to one another.

Finally, I told him why I had come: to meet him on behalf of a friend (whom I would not name), in hopes of learning more about his family and his circumstances. He continued to eye me suspiciously.

He would tell me only what I already knew: that he had been married to a woman who bore him two daughters, that he owned many cattle and sheep, and that his business employed about twenty workers, including six slaves. When I ventured to ask him how he acquired his land, he stood up with eyes flashing and told me that our interview was over.

How am I to interpret this? What shall I say to Mara? Should I counsel her to accept the other suitor, this Iddo, who is a harmless fellow and would never deceive her? Yet he has his faults too, as I learned from his sister. He is too generous (if that can be a fault); he gives away whatever money he happens to have with him. Other members of his family have tried to hide away some of the revenues he earns, but without success. His sister has become so exasperated by his behavior that she refuses to do business with him—she goes to another leather shop! Nevertheless, it is clear that she has a great deal of sisterly affection for him.

It seems that the choice comes down to this: a scoundrel or a fool. What else is left in Jerusalem, now that our best people have been taken to Babylon? Mara's choice reveals Yahweh's judgment on our nation, the inevitable fate of a sinful people.

Sixth month (2)
6th year Zedekiah

Diary entry:

Mara told me she could no longer put off her decision. She felt bad, she said, keeping the innocent Iddo in suspense any longer. So she told him no. The other man, Zaccai, has been urgent in his entreaties, and I suspect she was growing tired of fending him off. She has decided to accept his offer of marriage, but for the wrong reasons. She is fond of his little girls and says they need a mother. I begged her to wait until I could find out more about him, but she said no, her mind was made up.

I knew I had to act quickly. Early this morning I went to the house of Zaccai. I pounded on the door. He came quickly and opened it and told me to stop making such a racket lest I wake his children. I was not overly polite as I followed him into the hallway.

"I am here on urgent business."

"Yes, I can see that."

"You know a woman named Mara?"

"Yes, and what if I do?"

I grabbed the collar of his robe and pulled him close to my face, looking straight into his eyes.

"She is an honorable woman who deserves an honorable husband."

He tried to free himself from my grip, but I held tightly to his garment with trembling hands and began my accusation:

"You are reported by members of your own family to be a swindler, and there is nothing I can do about that. But I must have your promise that you will be a faithful husband to Mara, that you will never mistreat her or lie to her. And if I should find out otherwise, I will see that you are held accountable."

He seemed shocked by my speech, whether because of the accusation or because he learned for the first time that Mara would accept his proposal. At any rate, he could not answer immediately. When he did, his voice quavered.

"I see, sir, that you have some interest in Mara, and I suspect she is more to you than just a friend. Be that as it may, I will tell you something I rarely speak of outside the family, if you will only let go of me."

I loosened my grip.

"My brother is mentally unstable. Yes, it is true that I took his land, but only after he agreed that I should do so. When he is lucid, he knows I can manage the land better than he can, but sometimes he rants about it, claiming I stole it from him. Even worse are the accusations of his wife, who bitterly complains that I have cheated her son. This son is a young man who already shows signs of his father's instability. I have given them a house on the farm with servants and a man to watch over my brother so he doesn't harm himself. Naturally I have tried to keep them away from my children and my acquaintances in the city. Would you do otherwise?"

I said nothing, waiting for him to continue.

Finally he gave me his word that he would be a faithful husband. He swore he would speak only the truth to Mara. That is the best I could have expected.

Yet I know of someone who would make a better husband for her, if only the Lord willed it.

Dear Uncle Shallum,

Ever since you told me that the Hebrew scribes in Babylon had been writing the history of our people, I have been going over in my mind those ancient events that made us who we are. I am trying to determine how our history affects us today and whether the Jewish people are fulfilling their role as Yahweh's chosen ones.

The Lord made promises to Abraham, that his offspring would become a great and mighty nation, and all the other nations of the earth would be blessed through him. This promise was part of a covenant Yahweh made with Abraham, charging him to teach his children and his household to keep the ways of the Lord by doing righteousness and justice. Furthermore, Yahweh told Abraham that the covenant with him and his descendants would be an everlasting covenant.

Is it still valid? Can it be revoked? The people have been faithful in keeping one sign of the covenant, that is, circumcising every male child in the flesh of his foreskin when he is eight days old. But there is more! The other obligations of the covenant, namely righteousness and justice, are not practiced with such diligence.

Our history teaches us that sinfulness has penalties. When the men of Sodom sinned, the entire city went up in flames, and innocent people perished along with the guilty ones; even the pleading of Abraham could not save them. My pleading also seems to be in vain and my warnings of impending destruction fall on deaf ears.

Baruch recorded these lines of poetry which apparently came out of my mouth late one night when I was feeling despondent:

> *My anguish, my anguish! I writhe in pain!*
> *Oh, the walls of my heart!*
> *My heart is beating wildly; I cannot keep silent;*
> > *for I hear the sound of the trumpet, the alarm of war.*
> *Disaster follows hard on disaster, the whole land is laid waste.*
> *Suddenly my tents are destroyed, my curtains in a moment.*
> > *How long must I see the standard, and hear the sound of the trumpet?*

The outcome in Judah may be as terrible as the destruction of Sodom; if so, innocent people will suffer once again. The Lord later showed me this vision, which I hope will never come to pass:

I looked on the earth, and lo, it was waste and void;
  and to the heavens, and they had no light.
I looked on the mountains, and lo, they were quaking,
  and all the hills moved to and fro.
I looked, and lo, there was no man,
  and all the birds of the air had fled.
I looked, and lo, the fruitful land was a desert,
  and all its cities were laid in ruins
  before the Lord, before his fierce anger.

Our historians tell us that even after Sodom was destroyed, men in other cities remained faithful to the covenant, and the Lord kept all his promises. Many years later, the Lord promised King David that his descendants would rule Israel for as long as the kingdom endured, more years than men will be able to count. Will this promise be kept as well? Thus far, the line of David has endured for many generations, up to our present king Zedekiah. I wonder sometimes if this king is worthy of that lineage, to carry on the work of our great king David.

The king's behavior lately has been irrational, to say the least. In court last week, he acted like a petulant child, stamping his foot, pointing his finger, and calling people silly names. I did not escape his outburst; he called me something like "Tall-and-skinny Not-my-prophet" and made a public show of sending me out of the court. The ridicule did not trouble me, but I was disturbed by what happened in court after I was ejected.

My friend Shaphan told me afterwards that King Zedekiah had allowed molten images of calves to be brought before his throne. The king and several of his princes bowed themselves before the calves and offered sacrifices to them. No wonder he wanted me out of the court!

To make things worse, the king came to find me later in the temple and tried to justify his behavior. He actually offered me a string of shiny, colored jewels, and he attempted to win back my favor with sweet talk and promises of fidelity to the Lord Yahweh. How can he be so fickle?

The history of Israel (right up to the present day) has been a series of betrayals and returns to Yahweh. Happily, the Lord is never capricious like his people; he is a living God who sees everything and remembers good and evil, and who acts to protect, to save, and to punish his people. In the end, though, I fear he will lose patience with us.

Keep me informed, please, about the work of your scribes and what effect the historical writings have on the Jews in Babylon.

JEREMIAH with Baruch

First month
7th year in the reign
of King Zedekiah

My dear Uncle,

Ever since I sent my last letter to you, I have worried that it might cause you undue anxiety. Let me explain how my dreams and visions have affected me, and then perhaps they will seem less mysterious and frightful to you.

When I spoke of my anguish, I must have been thinking of my bowels, which always tie themselves in knots when I am agitated. You know that my physical reactions to emotional distress have always been extreme. My stomach becomes upset, my bowels evacuate, my heart beats wildly, and my breathing becomes quick.

These unpleasant symptoms came most recently in response to certain pictures running through my head: houses and tents collapsing, jars smashed, curtains torn in two, accompanied by the sound of shouting soldiers, thundering horses, and blaring trumpets. The visions became even more horrifying when the creation story came into my mind, and all the Lord's creative acts were reversed. The earth was once again waste and void and no lights lit up the heavens. The mountains quaked, the hills trembled, and all men and living things disappeared. It was an appalling vision, a return to chaos and darkness that prevailed before the Lord created the heavens and the earth.

Will the Lord allow this to happen? Perhaps he will not. Perhaps it is only a warning that the people must repent and return to him. Yet, if they do not return, then instead of protecting Israel, the Lord will declare war on her. His purpose will be firm and resistance will be useless. They will no more be able to escape his wrath than they can turn away the hot, sandy wind coming off the desert that dries up everything in its path.

How can Yahweh destroy his own people? He cares about them; this he has amply demonstrated again and again, over many centuries. Therefore, because he cares, he cannot let them go so wrong. It is necessary that they be defeated, and even destroyed, so that the land be purified and the remnant of Israel can begin again.

It all makes sense to me now, but it was horrifying to see these things in my mind's eye. You must not fret yourself about my loose bowels.

Shalom from
JEREMIAH (Baruch)

Diary entry:

Mara is married. Even during the betrothal I held out hope that her nuptial agreement would be revoked, but now it is too late. The decision is made, for better or for worse.

Her name is bitter in my mouth, like the herbs tasted by our fathers as they wandered in the desert. Now when I see Mara in the city, I will admire her from a distance, bitterly reminded that I am not to marry or to love any woman as my wife.

The Lord has surely spoken to me:

"You shall not take a wife, nor shall you have sons or daughters in this place. For thus says the Lord concerning the sons and daughters who are born in this place, and concerning the mothers who bore them and the fathers who begot them in this land: They shall die of deadly diseases. They shall not be lamented, nor shall they be buried; they shall be as dung on the surface of the ground. They shall perish by the sword and by famine, and their dead bodies shall be food for the birds of the air and for the beasts of the earth."

These words are a sign and a warning of the terrible anger of the Lord toward his people. I am called to be a witness, and thus will be compelled to watch things I would rather not see.

In forbidding me to marry, Yahweh has very likely spared me the pain of seeing my own family perish before my eyes. Yet, I think I would have taken that risk, had it been offered.

My dear Uncle,

I am alone. Ever since Yahweh spoke to me, saying that I should not take a wife nor should I have sons and daughters, ever since then I have looked at people differently, through new eyes. They are somehow removed from me, kept at arm's length where I cannot quite reach them. My heart aches when I see lovers walking hand in hand, or a little child dissolved in laughter as its father cuddles and tickles and teases it. The joy of family life will never be mine. There is an emptiness in my breast, Uncle, of which I am constantly reminded. When I am near others, their familiar chatter and affectionate glances inflict fresh wounds; when I am alone, the silence and emptiness of my house are overwhelming.

Intensifying my sense of separation from the people is the feeling that many of them now regard me as a traitor. Even my friends denounce me and look for opportunities to undermine my work. Do they imagine that I do not love the Hebrew nation with all my heart? You know that I do, Uncle. It is because I love them that I tell them they must repent of their evil ways. If they continue to worship false gods, to mistreat the poor and powerless, to defraud their neighbors, and to reject the laws of Yahweh, all the while paying lip service to religion and acting pious at the temple, then they will bring destruction upon themselves. Already, Yahweh has sent warnings; the army of Nebuchadnezzar has come down from the north to punish this people. Do they listen? Are they ashamed? Not in the slightest! These people have forgotten how to blush.

"For my people are foolish, they know me not;
they are stupid children, they have no understanding.
They are skilled in doing evil,
but how to do good they know not."

Is it too late? I do not know. Perhaps there will come a time when the people will have walked so far on the path to destruction that it will be too late for them to turn back.

"Can the Ethiopian change his skin or the leopard his spots?
Then also you can do good who are accustomed to do evil."

For now, I tell the people they must submit to the army of Nebuchadnezzar; that is clearly the fate Yahweh has ordained for them. Is this treason? No! It would be treason if I told them everything was all right and urged them to persist in their foolish ways which are in opposition to the purposes of Yahweh.

Nevertheless, people resent me. They want me to shut my mouth or, better yet, to disappear. *You* know that I cannot shut my mouth, for if I do, then there is a burning in my chest which compels me to speak. I hear people whisper that some of my enemies would like to harm me, to take revenge on me and to silence me. Yet I know the Lord is with me, so (most of the time) I am not afraid.

Uncle, it is a sad and lonely life which has been given me. Sometimes I wish to live as other people do, to be loved and esteemed by men—and women! However, I have willingly accepted a vocation which brings sadness and scorn.

Now that I have discharged my complaints on your long-suffering ears, I have a message to give you. I saw my kinsman Avi in the city yesterday. He told me of an incident long ago that sealed his affection and regard for your daughter. You remember Avi, perhaps, as a shy little boy who stammered and dragged one foot behind him as he walked. The village boys used to follow after him, imitating his gait, which brought him to tears on many occasions.

One day, when Avi was about seven years old, he and Orpah were leaving the market with their hands full of sweet dried fruits. The village rascals were lying in wait. They fell behind Avi in parade formation, as usual, but on that day he particularly did not wish to be followed. He began to run, loping clumsily like a cork bobbing in water. Orpah called for him to stop, but he kept running until his feet became tangled and he fell on his face. The apricots and raisins and dates flew out of his hands, into a pile of moist dung. Avi's elbows were scratched and bleeding, but he did not cry. He simply stood up and stared at his precious fruit. Orpah was behind him, and though Avi did not turn around, he could hear her scold the offending boys as if she had been their mother. She was a tiny little thing at the time, probably no more than five years old. After a few minutes she walked up behind Avi and touched his back. When he looked around, her hands were stretched out, offering her fruits to him. Avi told me that only then did he start to cry.

As Avi related this story to me, tears came again to his eyes. He asked me to send his affectionate greetings to you both and a kiss on the lips to Orpah.

You see the picture is not quite as bleak as I painted at the beginning of this letter; I am not always lonely. Baruch is with me when I need him, and I have other friends whom I love dearly. (Even a few family members are still speaking to me!) And yet, sometimes the tears will flow in spite of myself, as they have done today while I dictated this letter.

Remember always to cherish Orpah, your daughter and my cousin, for she is your greatest blessing.

My love to you both,
JEREMIAH by Baruch

Sixth month
7th year Zedekiah

Diary entry:

Now that I know the Lord does not wish for me to marry and have children, my line is ended; there is no one to keep my name alive after I am dead. Will the memory of me be blotted out? If I die tomorrow, will anyone carry on my work?

I must depend entirely on the Lord. He has tied me to himself in fetters tighter than a marriage bond. Dare I presume he will provide off-spring for me? Is it possible that his words spoken through my mouth will endure, taking the place of sons I will never have? Ha! That seems most unlikely, as I am not welcomed to speak and can hardly get a hearing any-where. No one will hear and therefore no one will remember. If, indeed, a calamity is coming, if an invasion brings total collapse of this nation, then the words I have preached will vanish as completely as the fog of the morning is burned away.

Baruch has proposed writing another scroll. He says if we write the words down and place them in a jar, someone may find them. After all, he pointed out, Moses wrote the Lord's words and they were preserved. This made me angry; I asked him again why he persists in comparing me to Moses. Anyone who found a scroll dictated by me would probably burn it, just as King Jehoiakim did many years ago.

Nevertheless, I will do as Baruch suggests. What else can I do? The Lord has made me an outcast, unmarried and forbidden even to attend weddings and funerals. It is only natural that the people should think me strange and stay away from me. I have little hope that the words I speak will be remembered, even though they are not my words, but the Lord's. He did promise once to put his words in my mouth.

*Eighth month
7th year in the reign
of King Zedekiah*

My dearest Uncle,

How long has it been since we greeted each other with a kiss? Eight years? It seems like a lifetime. I have grown old since I last saw you, both from the passing of years and from the burdens I must bear.

Uncle, it is not so much for myself that I weep as for this stiff-necked people who will not listen to any kind of warning. They have put their trust entirely in the accumulation of silver and gold, or in the temple cer-emonies and sacrifices, or in their own clever wits and strong bodies. Only in desperation (and sometimes not even then) will they listen to the words of the prophets of Yahweh.

Let me illustrate what I mean. Just last week in the market place, I witnessed an abomination. A woman approached a grain booth with five small, raggedy children trailing behind her. She laid her money on the table and asked for six omers of barley. The tradesman behind the table took a jar and measured out six omers. All of a sudden, one of the little children cried out in pain. As its mother turned around to tend to it, the scoundrel behind the counter reached into the jar, took back a handful of grain, and put sand in its place. Then he quickly poured it all into her sack and, before she turned around, tied it shut. I saw the scoundrel wink at his partner who was standing nearby holding a pea shooter which he had used, I believe, to shoot the child and thereby distract the mother.

The woman gathered her children and herded them away. I stood for a moment watching them before anger overtook me. I ran to the grain booth and demanded to know why they would cheat a poor woman and her children of their meager allotment of grain. I shook my fist at them. Do you know what they did? They laughed at me! They told me they would offer an extra pigeon at the temple. Remember the words of Hosea?

> *What shall I do with you, O Ephraim?*
> *What shall I do with you, O Judah?*
> *Your love is like a morning cloud, like the dew that goes early away.*
> *Therefore I have hewn them by the prophets,*
> *I have slain them by the words of my mouth,*
>   *and my judgment goes forth as the light.*
> *For I desire steadfast love and not sacrifice,*
>   *the knowledge of God, rather than burnt offerings.*

If these men knew the sacred writings, they would recognize their sin; but they are ignorant of scripture, all of them. Do you understand, Uncle, why I despair for this people?

JEREMIAH
by the hand of Baruch

Second month
8th year in the reign
of King Zedekiah

Dear Uncle,

Your last letter confirmed what I had suspected—some of your letters are not reaching me. I suppose this is inevitable, considering the great distance and treacherous terrain between us. Do you think it possible that the missing letters were confiscated by the Babylonians?

At any rate, I would like to hear about your sabbath observances in Babylon, which you had apparently described in a letter that was lost. Also, tell me more about the work of the scribes who are living with you in exile; I am encouraged that they are putting down in writing so much of our history and our law and our wisdom sayings, which the people are prone to forget.

The old man Shaphan still remembers! He stood in the inner court of the temple a few days ago and recited a psalm of David which has always been one of my favorites:

> *The law of the Lord is perfect, reviving the soul;*
>> *the testimony of the Lord is sure, making wise the simple;*
>> *the precepts of the Lord are right, rejoicing the heart;*
>> *the commandment of the Lord is pure, enlightening the eyes;*
>> *the fear of the Lord is clean, enduring for ever;*
>> *the ordinances of the Lord are true, and righteous altogether.*
> *More to be desired are they than gold, even much fine gold;*
>> *sweeter also than honey and drippings of the honeycomb.*

The temple officials usually allow me to stand and listen, but they become agitated if I open my mouth. I am not the only one forbidden to speak in the house of the Lord; anyone who pleads on behalf of the poor and powerless is silenced.

I am reminded of what the prophet Ezekiel said when he was still in Jerusalem, that the shepherds of Israel look after only themselves; they make no attempt to help the weak, the sick, or the lost. Nothing has changed since then. The priests think that burnt offerings and guilt offerings will absolve them of their sins and shortcomings. Can they not see that acts of penance are useless without a change of heart and a change of behavior? Those who truly love the Lord practice mercy and justice and do good works.

Why am I preaching to you, Uncle? There is nothing I can say that you do not already know.

I did want to ask your advice on a question raised by some dear friends of mine. A woman named Mara recently gave birth to a son. He is a lovely boy, lusty and vigorous. The woman also has two stepdaughters whom she loves dearly, but one of them is possessed by a demon. The little girl falls down and trembles, and her eyes roll back in her head. It is frightful to watch, yet Mara remains calm and even holds the girl in her arms while she convulses. Now Mara is worried that the demon may affect her son. Is the boy in danger? Do you know of a cure for the girl's affliction? If you have any healing balms or herbs which might help, please send them to me. I have prayed for her in the temple, but so far to no avail. I am afraid my prayers are not offered in the right spirit, because I see my enemies all around me, polluting the house of the Lord, and I become resentful.

JEREMIAH by the hand of Baruch

My poor, dear Uncle,

There is nothing, absolutely nothing, I can say that will make your grief easier to bear. You have lost your child, and no one can share in the agony you are suffering. That she should be struck down this way is incomprehensible; one so virtuous and full of vitality deserves to live. Why does the Lord allow a poisonous snake to attack a healthy young woman, cherished by all who know her?

Orpah was a flower in bloom. The last time I saw her, she was not much more than a child, yet already she was showing what sort of woman she would be. Her modesty and gravity were charming, and it was plain to all that she loved her father dearly. I know from your letters that she blossomed into a beautiful young woman, cheerfully attentive to your needs, even under the difficult conditions you encountered living in exile.

I am trying to imagine, dear Uncle, what it must be like to lose one's daughter, and worse yet, to stand by helplessly and watch her die. Perhaps it is like having a piece of your heart cut out, with the wound left open forever. I know I would be broken-hearted if Baruch died—he is almost like a son to me, even though we are nearly the same age. Yet Orpah was the flesh of your flesh and the image of her mother who was so dear to us all.

Yahweh is cruel. Why should you be punished while the wicked prosper? Why are the innocent afflicted with incurable wounds? I can only conclude that Yahweh is cruel.

With all my heart, I wish you a peaceful rest.
JEREMIAH with Baruch

Diary entry:

Is there no justice? Has the Lord abandoned his chosen ones? Are we merely playthings for Yahweh to amuse himself? So it seems.

This morning I stood in the temple and shouted at the Lord.

Why does the way of the wicked prosper?
Why do all who are treacherous thrive?
Thou plantest them, and they take root;
　　they grow and bring forth fruit;
　　thou art near in their mouth and far from their heart.

I know I created a stir, shouting as I did. The temple security officers were moving to take me away, but luckily for me, the old man Shaphan was there. Stooped with age but still full of dignity, he walked over and assured the officers that he would take care of me. The temple officials and priests all think I have gone mad, and who knows? Maybe I have.

I feel that the Lord has deceived me. He has made me a laughing-stock, a target of constant ridicule. When I predict violence and destruction for the city, the people laugh because they have heard it all before and it has not happened. The words that the Lord tells me to speak bring only disgrace and discredit to the speaker.

> *Cursed be the day on which I was born!*
> *The day when my mother bore me, let it not be blessed!*
> *Cursed be the man who brought the news to my father,*
> *"A son is born to you," making him very glad.*
> *Let that man be like the cities which the Lord overthrew without pity;*
> > *let him hear a cry in the morning and an alarm at noon,*
> > *because he did not kill me in the womb;*
> > *so my mother would have been my grave,*
> > *and her womb for ever great.*
> *Why did I come forth from the womb to see toil and sorrow,*
> > *and spend my days in shame?*

Seventh month
8th year Zedekiah

Diary entry:

I am ashamed of myself. Last night I ran out in the street and shouted like a madman. Earlier in the evening, I had been sitting in my house, full of anxiety and unable to sleep. As I was stewing over the wickedness of men, wondering why Yahweh does not bring punishment where it is deserved, my temper boiled over. I demanded to know why there is no justice. The Lord did not answer me. Grinding my teeth and pounding my fist, I asked Yahweh why he did not assert his sovereignty. Still there was no answer.

Then I went outside and grabbed the first person I saw. He broke free, but not until he had endured a loud and obnoxious (and probably undeserved) tirade from me. I stopped others on the street and shouted at them. One of them shouted back, "You don't even know me," which was true. Others made ugly faces at me and threatened me physically. Finally I retreated into my house, exhausted.

Now I feel terrible about losing my temper and my self-control. I hesitate to show my face outside, for fear people will taunt me. If there were some way to express my regret, I would. But I could never recognize the people I confronted; even if it had been light outside, I was in such a froth I could not see straight. It is useless.

How can I communicate the word of the Lord so that the wayward people of this land will not be cast away as refuse? They are like a wife whose husband is disgusted by her lewd behavior. Suppose the husband sends her away with a certificate of divorce and she marries another man, and that man also divorces her. Should the first husband take her back again? Moses says this would be an abomination, a stain upon the whole land. Yet Israel has played the harlot with many lovers, and the land is greatly polluted. Can she still expect her first husband Yahweh to take her back?

The Lord, her first husband, cannot be appeased with fertility rituals or harvest bribes. Baal's favor can be bought, but Yahweh has greater expectations. He wants our hearts and minds, our steadfast loyalty, and our obedience to his covenant laws.

The prophet Hosea knew Israel for a harlot when he spoke the word of the Lord:

> "Plead with your mother, plead—
> for she is not my wife, and I am not her husband—
> that she put away her harlotry from her face,
> and her adultery from between her breasts;
> For their mother has played the harlot;
> she that conceived them has acted shamefully.
> For she said, 'I will go after my lovers,
> who give me my bread and my water, my wool and my flax,
> my oil and my drink.'
> Therefore I will hedge up her way with thorns;
> and I will build a wall against her, so that she cannot find her paths.
> She shall pursue her lovers, but not overtake them;
> and she shall seek them, but shall not find them.
> Then she shall say, 'I will go and return to my first husband,
> for it was better with me then than now.'
> And she did not know that it was I who gave her the grain,
> the wine, and the oil,
> and who lavished upon her silver and gold which they used for Baal."

The people who heard Hosea prophesy probably took him for a madman. Now my compatriots think I am deranged and will have nothing to do with me. I may as well be a leper, living alone outside the camp and crying "unclean" when anyone approaches.

Eighth month
8th year Zedekiah

Diary entry:

The sword of the Lord has been given a mission—why has it not been drawn from its scabbard? A lion has gone forth from its den—why has it not devoured its prey?

The Lord seduced me. He made me believe that Judah would be punished, in the same way the northern tribes were punished by the Assyrians a hundred years ago. Yet he allowed Judah to survive the Assyrian invaders, and now he lets people believe the temple will protect them from the Babylonians as well. I have been tricked by the Lord; he has left me alone to fend for myself. His last word to me was derision:

> *"If you have raced with men on foot, and they have wearied you,*
> *how will you compete with horses?*
> *And if in a safe land you fall down,*
> *how will you do in the jungle of the Jordan?"*

Although it seems impossible, the Lord is telling me that things will get worse. So far, I have tried to live righteously and have refrained from breaking the law. Now I find myself tempted to curse my parents and to utter an oath against the Lord. Then, according to the law of Moses, I should be put to death and this miserable life would be ended, once and for all.

The Lord knows I have not desired the day of disaster nor pressed him to send evil to this land. Everything that comes out of my lips came first from his mouth. The people scoff at me and ask, "Where is the judgment of the Lord? Let it come!" so now, if the Lord still hears my prayers, I will ask him to put them to shame, to destroy them once and for all.

The choice comes to me again, whether I should follow the Lord's commands that lead nowhere or hide myself away and do nothing. The result is the same either way.

Tenth month
8th year in the reign
of King Zedekiah

Dearest Uncle,

I hope that the passage of time has blunted the sharp pain of your loss. Yahweh does indeed have some things to answer for.

Over the last few months, since receiving word of Orpah's death, I have been considering the question: Do the memories of joyful times counterbalance the pain of loss? Is each man a scale, who, when given his portions of good and evil, must balance them on his shoulders, or else topple over into despair? No, this is not right. The scale will not balance. There is no compensation for the loss you have suffered.

What are we to conclude—that a life such as yours is not worth living? Absolutely not! You have loved and been loved. I would gladly give half the years of my life to know the love you have known. Life is sweet and bitter, all of a piece.

I have spoken my mind to Yahweh; he never fails to speak back. Once again, he has taught me a lesson in humility, telling me that until I see the glory of the Lord (as Moses did while he was standing in the cleft of the rock), I cannot know his unsearchable ways. Some day, perhaps, men will understand, but not until the Lord wills it.

To give you some idea of what is going on here in Jerusalem, the priests and prophets continually argue with one another, and most of them give bad advice to the king. They are so thick-headed that I am forced to play games and tricks if I wish to make a point. One day I brought jars to the court and filled them with wine. I told the people that if they kept arguing with each other and acting stupid, as if they were drunk, the Lord would dash them one against the other and destroy them all. Naturally, I dashed the jars together and made quite a mess on the floor.

Do you think they listened? No, they continued to counsel alliance with Egypt and rebellion against Babylon, and they nearly convinced King Zedekiah to withhold tribute from King Nebuchadnezzar.

The strain of my work (added to personal sorrow) has taken its toll on this old body. You would hardly recognize me now: My hair is completely white and rather wild-looking (or so I am told by my friends). I am thinner than before and my shoulders are stooped, but nevertheless I still stand a head taller than most of the people around me. My cheeks are sunken and my sharp facial bones protrude under grizzled eyebrows. You probably remember my long spidery fingers—some people think I am spinning a web to catch the king and those of his advisers who disagree with me.

Baruch is with me now in my house, writing as I dictate. My room is just as sparsely furnished as when you were here, containing only a desk with an oil lamp, a stool, and a sleeping mat. Baruch sits at the desk while I pace up and down the room thinking about what I should say to you at a time like this, knowing that nothing I say will comfort you in your time of mourning. Perhaps I should describe my domestic situation.

My old cook and housekeeper, Sarai, is still with me. Her husband lives here too; he has become lame in his old age and can no longer do heavy labor as he used to do, or even tend the garden beside the house. He now sits quietly most days mending clothes and shoes for this household and others nearby. Their room contains a few more "luxury" items than mine, such as a table with a wash basin, shelves for storing mats and cloths, and a seat lined with animal skins. But for the most part, we live a simple life, much as you did years ago in Anathoth.

I wish you were here, Uncle. Write to me again and tell me all the wonderful things you remember about your daughter. Then I, too, will know her as the woman who began to fulfill the promise of the little girl.

Jehudi and others in the court send their greetings and condolences.

Your loving nephew JEREMIAH

with Baruch

Despair

Dearest Uncle Shallum,

I wish you were here. I long to sit down with you and talk for many hours as we used to do, about things which disturbed and perplexed us, and also about things which inspired our hopes. But you are not here, so I will do my best to give you my part of the discussion in writing and then wait patiently for your response. The great distance between us is forcing me to learn patience!

On the hopeful side, a young Babylonian soldier named Zerubbaz has become my disciple! He spends his free time with me, studying Torah and soaking up everything I teach him about the law and the prophets. He is not yet twenty years old but shows unusual perceptiveness and wisdom for one so young.

Even so, I was not prepared for what happened last week; in fact, I am still amazed when I think of it. Zerubbaz approached me early one morning as I was going to pray at the temple. He clearly had something he wanted to say to me, but could not get the words out. After shifting from one foot to the other and hesitating so long I thought I would miss my morning prayers, he finally told me he wanted to embrace the Hebrew faith! He said he felt sure that the Lord Yahweh is the one true God who made heaven and earth; and if it were required that he undergo ritual cleansing and circumcision before he be allowed to worship Yahweh, he said he was willing.

I didn't know quite how to answer, so I told Zerubbaz I would look into it. In the meanwhile, I told him to keep studying Torah and try to live according to the precepts of the law.

When I arrived at the temple, I spoke with a couple of priests, hinting that it might happen some day that one of our Babylonian visitors would convert to Judaism. I was hoping to find out their ideas on the subject, and I did. Once they realized what I was saying, they howled with laughter. It is manifestly clear to me that Zerubbaz's inquiry will get no serious consideration from the officials now ruling the temple.

Now, Uncle, I want to hear what you think about this. Is it wise for me to help this man become a Jew? How should I proceed? Who is likely to help me or to sabotage my efforts?

The other issue I wanted to discuss with you falls into the category labeled "disturbing and disheartening." As I observe the people around me, I have been counting in my mind the number of transgressions against the ten commandments brought by Moses. In just one month, I have seen with my own eyes people stealing, committing adultery, swearing falsely, dishonoring their parents, and, most frequently of all, worshipping false gods. That makes five that I could see! In all likelihood, the other five are broken just as often.

As to the case of adultery which I saw, I would rather not describe it to you, except to say it was quite disgusting and within earshot of my house. I will tell you, though, about the contemptuous treatment of an elderly man and his wife by their own son.

Baruch and I were invited to dine with the elderly couple one evening. While we were eating, the son burst into the house, and, without so much as a word of greeting, ordered his father to get up from the table.

"Can't you see we have guests, my son?" asked the father.

"I see what I see," was the impudent answer.

"But what do you wish to say?"

"I want to speak to you in private."

As he said this, he lifted the old man bodily from his seat and ushered him into the next room. We heard animated conversation and what sounded like threats from the son.

When he returned to the table, the old man was rather quiet and downcast. We learned from him later, as we conversed after dinner, that his son was in debt and had taken various items of value from his parents' house. I presume that was the purpose of his latest visit.

Do such men as this not realize that their unrighteous actions bring condemnation and ruin upon the entire community? Their sins are like foul pus which spills out of a wound and infects all the people.

Now you know what I am thinking about. Please give me your opinions and insights on these matters, and reassure me that the Hebrew people in Babylon do not take the law so lightly.

JEREMIAH by Baruch

Fourth month
9th year Zedekiah

Diary entry:

Zerubbaz continues to astonish me. He comes to see me no less than twice each week to study the law and debate its meaning. Granted, he is a young man of rare intellect, but even so, his understanding and insight have grown faster than I could have imagined. He tells me he had not heard anything about Yahweh until he came to Jerusalem, and yet he seems to have some kind of innate knowledge of the one true God.

Our most recent discussion began with the psalms of David, and especially the parts where David praises the Lord for delivering him from his enemies. David says:

> *The Lord rewarded me according to my righteousness;*
> > *according to the cleanness of my hands he recompensed me.*
> *For I have kept the ways of the Lord,*
> > *and have not wickedly departed from my God.*

and again:

> *I was blameless before him, and I kept myself from guilt.*
> *Therefore the Lord has recompensed me according to my righteousness,*
> > *according to the cleanness of my hands in his sight.*

In our discussion, Zerubbaz expressed misgivings, not about King David himself or his worthiness before the Lord, but about other equally good men who seem not to reap the benefits of the Lord's favor. He asked how this could happen. If Yahweh is just and good and all-knowing, why is it that a diligent man sometimes strives all his life to achieve a goal and then loses everything in an instant? How can it happen that honest men remain poor, while cheaters gain riches? Why do the righteous and the wicked all come to the same fate in the end?

Our discussion went on for hours. Of course, I could not answer all his questions, but we talked about different kinds of rewards besides material goods, such as a clear conscience, a good night's sleep, companionship with like-minded people, and real enjoyment of life's small pleasures. Perhaps righteousness does not guarantee visible rewards, but nevertheless, doing one's duty has certain compensations of its own.

I find these discussions exhausting, but Zerubbaz wants to talk on and on, late into the night. During our sessions, his bright eyes open wider and wider, and his lean body becomes animated as he gestures with his hands and occasionally jumps from his seat in his excitement. He is a handsome lad with straight black hair and a strong, high-bridged nose. His dark eyes are shaded by long, thick eyelashes, but his beard is (as yet) rather light.

I interrupted our theological discussion one night to ask if he thought the Babylonians had appointed a spy to follow me around. I explained (without giving too many details) that I had observed a white-haired man watching me in different locales. Zerubbaz frowned at my question and said he thought it unlikely, since his compatriots generally regard me with approval, certainly not as an enemy. Then he steered the conversation back to more "interesting topics," as he put it.

I have even asked old Shaphan and his sons if they too are followed and watched. They thought not, but expressed concern that I had observed such activities. Perhaps they will overhear something from the temple authorities (who might be behind all this). If I knew who it was, I would be less disturbed.

Sixth month
9th year in the reign
of King Zedekiah

Dear Uncle Shallum,

My hope is fading that the people of Judah will repent.

Other prophets from past generations warned that the northern kingdom of Israel would bring ruin upon itself by forsaking the Lord. You remember, Uncle, reading about how Israel played the harlot, and her people lusted after false gods. They mingled with cult prostitutes in pagan sanctuaries on hilltops and within sacred groves. The end came as the prophets said it would: The Assyrians marched against the northern kingdom and laid waste to the land. Cities became desolate piles of rubble.

The people in the south saw what happened, how the Lord sent Israel away with a decree of divorce, yet they chose to follow in the footsteps of their faithless sister. Judah has played the harlot with Baal and become thoroughly defiled. The Lord planted the best seeds for his vineyard but the vines grew wild.

> *Though you wash yourself with lye and use much soap,*
> *the stain of your guilt is still before me, says the Lord God.*
> *How can you say, "I am not defiled, I have not gone after the Baals"?*
> *Look at your way in the valley; know what you have done—*
> *a restive young camel interlacing her tracks,*
> *a wild ass used to the wilderness, in her heat sniffing the wind!*

Who can restrain her lust?
None who seek her need weary themselves;
*   in her month they will find her.*

At last I think I understand why the Lord has commanded me to cease praying for these people. They have hardened their hearts. Their corruption and self-deception have become ingrained; their willful disobedience has grown into the habit of sin. Yahweh's decision to punish the people is irrevocable, hence my prayers are in vain.

This word of the Lord came to me as I was praying late one night:

"Therefore do not pray for this people, or lift up a cry or prayer on their behalf, for I will not listen when they call to me in the time of their trouble. What right has my beloved in my house, when she has done vile deeds? Can vows and sacrificial flesh avert your doom? Can you then exult? The Lord once called you, 'A green olive tree, fair with goodly fruit'; but with the roar of a great tempest he will set fire to it, and its branches will be consumed. The Lord of hosts, who planted you, has pronounced evil against you, because of the evil which the house of Israel and the house of Judah have done, provoking me to anger by burning incense to Baal."

Nowhere else on the earth does disobedience prevail as it does with the sons of men. Swallows, storks and turtledoves know the proper times to fly away from this place and to come back. The sea does not pass its boundaries; the waves do not prevail against the land. Snow never leaves the peaks of Mt. Hermon and its cold, clear streams do not stop flowing.

Yet the sons of men, who think themselves wise, are unwise, and those who claim to know the law have made it into a lie. How can men be wise who have rejected the word of the Lord and perverted the law? It grieves me to say that these men will be put to shame. The Lord will send great afflictions for their chastisement.

I am glad you and the other exiles have been removed from this place so you need not witness the rottenness in Judah. By taking you far away, the Lord has preserved you from contamination. I believe some day the faithful remnant of Israel will return, but not until the Lord has accomplished his purpose to purify this land and the hearts of the people.

Be thankful, Uncle, that you have a secure home, well-fortified and protected against invasion. We feel ourselves to be less secure here, but we are reassured by your most recent letter that the faith of our fathers Abraham and Isaac is at least kept alive among the exiles in Babylon.
JEREMIAH by Baruch

Seventh month
9th year in the reign
of King Zedekiah

Dear Uncle,

Things are getting worse.

This city has become stained by the blood it has shed and defiled by the idols it has worshipped. It has become a reproach to all peoples, mocked by those who are near and those who are far. The Lord's name has been profaned in the sight of all the nations; but he will deal with us, and we will know that he is the Lord.

Every day I make mental entries into my catalogue of sins of the people, and with loathing I observe manifold transgressions against the commandments of Yahweh. For example, Moses bid us practice hospitality and justice toward strangers who sojourn in the land, and he declared that there be one law and one ordinance applied to natives and sojourners alike. Nevertheless, our people look for any excuse to threaten, intimidate, and cheat new immigrants of their wealth. To be sure, the people don't behave much better toward their fellow inhabitants of Jerusalem, but it seems they find more opportunities to swindle the foreigners who live among us.

An incident I heard about last month made my blood boil. A coppersmith from Egypt, a Jew, came to Jerusalem to sell his wares. This Egyptian, being a devout man, naturally made regular visits to the temple while he was staying in the city.

My friend Elasah (Shaphan's third son, do you remember?) was doing business in the outer court of the temple when the Egyptian came to make a transaction at the stall next to him. He wanted to buy a ram for sacrifice. Being unfamiliar with our system of weights, he pulled out a sack full of copper and silver bits and poured them on the table. When the man in the stall saw the shiny pieces of accumulated wealth, his eyes bulged. He laid a ten-shekel weight on the scale and balanced it with silver and copper pieces and took nearly the whole pile as payment.

Elasah knew that the Egyptian had paid five times the usual price for one ram, and he said as much out loud. The salesman in the stall scowled and told him to mind his own business, but Elasah persisted. When a priest approached, having heard the argument from across the courtyard, the salesman immediately appealed for arbitration. The priest heard the salesman's story and Elasah's objection; after pretending to deliberate for a few minutes, he said the payment was fair. With a wink of his eye, he told

Elasah that a foreigner's sacrifice might be less pleasing to the Lord unless he also made an offering for upkeep of the temple. Then he walked away.

The Egyptian coppersmith seemed somewhat confused by the whole transaction, since he did not understand the language perfectly. He shrugged his shoulders as he led his ram away.

After Elasah told me this story, I read to him the words I had dictated to Baruch not long ago:

> *From the least to the greatest of them,*
> *every one is greedy for unjust gain;*
> *and from prophet to priest, every one deals falsely.*

I have heard also of cases where our own widows and orphans were treated shamefully, stripped of their few possessions simply because they were too weak to resist. It is also reported that some men take payment to shed blood; others extort interest when they lend money.

The sins of sexual immorality are as common as the sins of avarice. Men commit lewd acts with ritual prostitutes in the high places of Baal. They uncover and ridicule their fathers' nakedness, and they have intercourse with women who are unclean in their time of impurity. One man sleeps with his neighbor's wife; another defiles his daughter-in-law; yet another commits abomination with his own sister, the daughter of his father. Can you believe the depravity of these people?

Our so-called leaders, the princes in Jerusalem, are like ravenous wolves tearing their prey, shedding blood and devouring human lives to get dishonest gain. They take treasures for themselves and make many widows in the land.

The priests, too, take part in this contemptible behavior. They despise the statutes and ignore the law. They make no distinction between the holy and the common or between the clean and the unclean. Worst of all, they lead the people to despise the holy things and to profane the sabbaths.

The Lord searches for a good man in Jerusalem as he searched in Sodom, so that he might have mercy on us.

> *Run to and fro through the streets of Jerusalem,*
> *look and take note!*
> *Search her squares to see if you can find a man,*
> *one who does justice and seeks truth;*
> *that I may pardon her.*

Because the people have refused to repent and have made their hearts harder than rock, the Lord will deal with them, and they will know that he is the Lord.

But what am I to do, Uncle? I try not to despair, but I find it nearly impossible to continue preaching and praying as the Lord commands me. I need your wise counsel more than ever.

JEREMIAH with Baruch

Eighth month
9th year in the reign
of King Zedekiah

Dear Uncle,

I feel in my bones that a great calamity is coming.

> *At the noise of horseman and archer every city takes to flight;*
> *they enter thickets; they climb among rocks;*
> *all the cities are forsaken, and no man dwells in them.*
> *And you, O desolate one, what do you mean that you dress in scarlet,*
> *that you deck yourself with ornaments of gold,*
> *that you enlarge your eyes with paint?*
> *In vain you beautify yourself.*
> *Your lovers despise you; they seek your life.*
> *For I heard a cry as of a woman in travail,*
> *anguish as of one bringing forth her first child,*
> *the cry of the daughter of Zion gasping for breath,*
> *stretching out her hands*
> *"Woe is me! I am fainting before murderers."*

These faithless people continue to run after false gods and fornicate with them. They grasp at one object of devotion after another but find nothing that satisfies, because they put their trust in the works of man and not in the Lord Yahweh. Do they think they can gain favor with powerful neighbors by pledging loyalty to their carved idols? Do they not realize that people who go after nothingness *become* nothing?

The king is no better than his fickle subjects. He desperately seeks to win the approval of others, especially those who promise him wealth and success. He wavers between weak allegiance to Yahweh and obeisance to other gods and men. I learned from a friend, who (unlike myself) is still permitted to attend political discussions in the court, that King Zedekiah has finally decided to withhold tribute from the Babylonians. Furthermore, says my friend, he has cemented a military alliance with Egypt against the

Babylonian army. If the alliance holds and if our foolish king publicly defies Nebuchadnezzar, he will have initiated our destruction. On this shaky foundation rests the fate of Israel.

The words I hear from the Lord are a fire in my mouth which will devour this people made of wood.

> *"Behold, I am bringing upon you a nation from afar,*
> *O house of Israel, says the Lord.*
> *It is an enduring nation, it is an ancient nation,*
> *a nation whose language you do not know,*
> *nor can you understand what they say.*
> *Their quiver is like an open tomb, they are all mighty men.*
> *They shall eat up your harvest and your food;*
> *they shall eat up your sons and your daughters;*
> *they shall eat up your flocks and your herds;*
> *they shall eat up your vines and your fig trees;*
> *your fortified cities in which you trust they shall destroy with the sword.*
> *But even in those days, says the Lord, I will not make a full end of you. And when your people say, 'Why has the Lord our God done all these things to us?' you shall say to them, 'As you have forsaken me and served foreign gods in your land, so you shall serve strangers in a land that is not yours.'"*

Uncle, the situation is grim. If only Zedekiah would give up his ideas of rebellion and surrender unconditionally to the Babylonians, then the Hebrew people would have a chance to survive in Jerusalem. But the king continues to ignore my counsel, even while he clings to me for good luck.

The king is not the only false shepherd in Jerusalem. An incident which occurred at the temple will give you indication of just how badly our religious leaders are conducting themselves.

Do you remember my writing to you about Zerubbaz, my young Babylonian friend who wants to be a Jew? You wrote back with good advice, which I acted upon and will tell you about presently.

Shortly after your letter arrived, I had a dream (at least, I think it was a dream) in which a man with gleaming white hair spoke to me from the balcony of a tower. He was too high up for me to see his lips moving or to hear what he said, yet I understood every word perfectly. He said the Lord would have compassion on our neighbors who worshipped Baal. He said if foreign nations will turn their allegiance to the Lord and live faithfully by his laws, even though they once enticed the Hebrew people to bow down to Baal, these foreigners will be accepted as the Lord's own people. I took this to be a message from Yahweh, confirming your advice regarding young Zerubbaz, and I decided then and there to do exactly as you advised.

One afternoon, when Zerubbaz had completed his watch duty by the Damascus Gate, we set out together, as you suggested, to find your old friend Jacob, learned priest and teacher of the law. We found him at home, where he stays most of the time on account of his advanced age and infirmities. After he asked a series of questions of the young soldier, the teacher said he was satisfied that this man was already a Jew in his heart and required only circumcision to become a Jew in actuality. He agreed to perform the circumcision ritual that same afternoon.

Zerubbaz was rather sore after it was done and had some difficulty walking. We arranged to meet your friend Jacob at the temple the next morning, and then I escorted the young man, slowly and carefully, back to his quarters.

The next morning he was feeling better. We set out for the temple, and on the way we met the old teacher hobbling along the road near the south wall. The three of us approached the gate of the outer courtyard, where we encountered a small contingent of temple officers. These were priests of the Lord, you understand.

My presence was probably a goad to provoke their hostility, but one would still expect these officers to show a little deference to an elderly and well-respected teacher and fellow priest. They did not. When Jacob explained that we had come to worship Yahweh in the temple, they laughed in his face. Perhaps suspecting a recent circumcision, one of them kicked Zerubbaz in the groin, where he was sore. The old teacher approached the man who had kicked our young friend and began to rebuke him, but he was rudely pushed to the ground for his trouble. Meanwhile, one of the other officers had grabbed my arms and twisted them behind my back to prevent my intervening.

They called me a traitor and told me to take this foreigner away from sacred ground. They warned Zerubbaz not to come near the temple again, or he would regret it. One of them spat on him.

Have these people not read the scriptures, where it says we are to accommodate foreigners who pray to the Lord? Perhaps I should remind them of Solomon's prayer at the dedication of the temple:

"Likewise when a foreigner, who is not of thy people Israel, comes from a far country for the sake of thy great name, and thy mighty hand, and thy outstretched arm, when he comes and prays toward this house, hear thou from

heaven thy dwelling place, and do according to all for which the foreigner calls to thee; in order that all peoples of the earth may know thy name and fear thee, as do thy people Israel, and that they may know that this house which I have built is called by thy name."

The Hebrew people and their leaders will be punished for this behavior. Yahweh has appointed the mighty army of Nebuchadnezzar to destroy the fortified cities of Judah, and Zerubbaz himself will have a hand in punishing his new brothers in faith.

I am beginning to feel as if a heavy weight presses on my head and shoulders. It gets harder each day for me to carry myself where I should go. Baruch stays faithfully at my side when he is not needed at home, but he cannot study and pray and teach for me, so my work remains unfinished.

If you can give me some reason to hope, I would be grateful.
JEREMIAH
with Baruch

Ninth month
9th year Zedekiah

Diary entry:

> *Judah mourns and her gates languish;*
> > *her people lament on the ground,*
> > *and the cry of Jerusalem goes up.*
> *Her nobles send their servants for water;*
> > *they come to the cisterns,*
> > *they find no water, they return with their vessels empty;*
> > *they are ashamed and confounded and cover their heads.*
> *Because of the ground which is dismayed,*
> > *since there is no rain on the land,*
> > *the farmers are ashamed, they cover their heads.*
> *Even the hind in the field forsakes her newborn calf*
> > *because there is no grass.*
> *The wild asses stand on the bare heights, they pant for air like jackals;*
> > *their eyes fail because there is no herbage.*

This is the word of the Lord which Baruch recorded on a scroll during the last famine, when thousands of people died. Though fifteen years have passed, I cannot forget the babies with sunken cheeks and sticks attached to their swollen bellies where arms and legs should have been. I watched them nurse frantically at the breasts of their bleary-eyed mothers, breasts which were as dry as the empty cisterns. Why did the Lord spare my life, my worthless life, when so many innocent people perished?

Now they suffer a different sort of drought, much worse than before. They have abandoned the fountain of living waters, their Lord Yahweh, and their souls will die along with their bodies.

Yet who am I to tell the people how to live their lives? I think that I hear Yahweh speaking and I am sure that I am following his commands. But in the end, nothing turns out right, no one listens, and my efforts are as fruitless as a dead fig tree. I am a worthless man whose claim to be a prophet is pure presumption; my self-assurance is only pride and vanity. I must be deceiving myself in claiming to be a prophet, for I do not listen to Yahweh, and Yahweh does not listen to me.

It has not always been so.

> *Thy words were found, and I ate them,*
> > *and thy words became to me a joy and the delight of my heart;*
> > *for I am called by thy name, O Lord, God of hosts.*
> *I did not sit in the company of merrymakers, nor did I rejoice;*
> *I sat alone, because thy hand was upon me,*
> > *for thou hadst filled me with indignation.*
> *Why is my pain unceasing, my wound incurable, refusing to be healed?*
> *Wilt thou be to me like a deceitful brook, like waters that fail?*

For three days and nights I have had the dreadful sensation that Yahweh has forsaken me; he has left me to suffer while he hides himself from me. In this state of mind, I find it difficult to hold a pen or to keep my hand steady.

When I close my eyes and try to rest, I see the dim shadow-figure pursuing me with a flaming torch. He presses me to keep climbing a steep, jagged mountain, though I am thirsty and exhausted. If I slow down to catch my breath, he approaches with the flame outstretched, so that my back and my head are burning.

When I wake from this uneasy sleep, I feel empty and without hope. All my energy is used up going over and over in my mind what I have said and done in the past. All my mistakes, my insufficient arguments, my poor judgments come rushing back into my head, and again and again I frantically repeat what I should have said and done in each situation.

I fear I might have died of thirst and despair, languishing in this hell of my own making, if Baruch had not come to me. Patiently, he sits with me for hours holding my hand and putting his arms around my chest when I begin to shake, and often he prays for me. There is not much else he can do except make me drink a little water, yet he stays at my side. This morning he read to me from the prophet Hosea. In my mental agitation, I could not comprehend the words he pronounced, but even so, I did not ask him to stop reading.

Tenth month
9th year Zedekiah

Diary entry:

For two weeks, I did not leave my house. In fact, most days I was not able to drag myself out of bed. With heart and mind in a state of agitation, I mulled over the wrongs committed against me by my enemies and my friends. I lashed out at Baruch when he tried to make me eat; at other times I disregarded him completely, even while he pleaded with me to tell him what he could do to help me.

During this time, the shadow figure visited me every day. He grew larger and uglier each time I saw him. Blood and flames poured from his nose and mouth as he paced frantically through the house. Now I realize I must have been hallucinating, because Baruch never saw him.

Looking back, I can see that I was in an agony of self-pity. Somehow, during those horrible two weeks, I was able to focus only on myself, believing the whole universe to be centered around me, and against me. By indulging in this grotesque fantasy, I sank further and further into my own miserable self and away from the world around me, until I was utterly helpless to pull myself out. The only help was to wait for the Lord.

The Lord is good to those who wait for him,
   to the soul that seeks him.
It is good that one should wait quietly
   for the salvation of the Lord.
For the Lord will not cast off for ever,
   but, though he cause grief,
   he will have compassion according to the abundance
   of his steadfast love;
   for he does not willingly afflict or grieve the sons of men.

Now I understand that Yahweh gave me this opportunity to know how very helpless and weak I am, just like any other man. At times, I am unable to govern my own thoughts and actions, though I know I am doing wrong. It is only on the strength of Yahweh that a man can depend, not on priests, princes, prophets, or even on himself. We are all sinful men, weak and unable to resist the temptation to disobey the Lord.

Until now I have taken pride in my own righteousness and self-mastery and also in my ability to influence others. I can no longer take pride in such things. Now I understand that my vocation as a prophet, and therefore my entire life, may end in failure. And yet, if I submit to the will of Yahweh and if I am faithful to his word, then my life will not be such a complete failure as it may appear. Success in the eyes of the world depends partly on accidents of chance and partly on the unpredictable responses of other men; surely a person will not be held accountable for outcomes which are beyond his control. I believe the Lord Yahweh demands faithfulness, but not success.

> *Therefore thus says the Lord:*
> *"If you return, I will restore you, and you shall stand before me.*
> *If you utter what is precious, and not what is worthless,*
> > *you shall be as my mouth.*
> *They shall turn to you, but you shall not turn to them."*

Now that I understand this, I feel the load on my back has been lightened. It is easier for me to prophesy once again, even though I face ridicule and scorn. Now I can confidently declare what the Lord has revealed to me: that catastrophe is waiting like a lion on its haunches just outside the gates of the city.

Tenth month
9th year in the reign
of King Zedekiah

Dear Uncle,

The siege has begun. The army of Nebuchadnezzar is surrounding Jerusalem and preparing to attack.

If we climb the city walls, we can see (or at least imagine that we see) the glint of swords and axes in the distant encampments. Horses carry men and materials back and forth to construction sites where huge wooden siegeworks are taking shape. Occasionally a group of chariots will approach one of the city gates and send a stream of arrows and spears toward our watchmen, and then retreat quickly behind their galloping horses. As they turn to flee, we can see that the chariot drivers are wearing helmets and heavy armor breastplates, and some of the riders carry half-shields or leather bucklers. This Babylonian army is well-trained and well-equipped—the very sight of them inspires fear in the hearts of our people, who wait like sheep for the day of slaughter.

Yesterday King Zedekiah sent two of his courtiers, asking me to inquire of the Lord Yahweh if he would do a marvelous work and make Nebuchadnezzar and his army go away. I said there was no chance of that.

I gave them this message to take back to the king: If he surrenders to Nebuchadnezzar his life will be spared and his honor upheld; but if not, the Lord of Israel says he will make useless the weapons of war with which the people of Jerusalem fight against the Chaldean army, and he will permit the army to overrun the city. The Lord himself will fight against the Hebrew people, his wrath and fury falling upon them like blows from a sword. As for King Zedekiah and his people who survive this warfare and also the disease and famine that follow, they will be delivered to the king of Babylon. He will have no pity on them but will hack them to pieces.

I also sent out a message to the people of Jerusalem: The Lord is giving you a choice between life and death. If you stay here, you will surely die from battle wounds, disease, or hunger; but if you surrender to the Chaldeans outside the city walls, you shall live. The city will be taken by King Nebuchadnezzar and he will burn it to the ground.

Perhaps I am foolish, Uncle, but I still hold a glimmer of hope that the people will do what is right. Yet I am reminded of the sign given me by Yahweh several years ago. (The whole thing was rather strange.) The Lord told me to take a clean, dry waistcloth that I had worn about my loins and bury it near the Euphrates River. So I carried the loincloth that had been on my body a great distance and hid it under a broken rock by the great river Euphrates.

Later the Lord told me to go back and retrieve the loincloth. When I dug it out of the ground it was, as you might imagine, filthy and slimy, no longer fit to be worn. Then the word of the Lord came to me:

Even so will I spoil the pride of Judah and the great pride of Jerusalem. This evil people, who refuse to hear my words, who stubbornly follow their own heart and have gone after other gods to serve them and worship them, shall be like this waistcloth, which is good for nothing. For as the waistcloth clings to the loins of man, so I made the whole house of Israel and the whole house of Judah cling to me, says the Lord, that they might be for me a people, a name, a praise, and a glory, but they would not listen.

Some of them seem to be listening now, though, inspired by the immense army at our doorstep. This army will undoubtedly teach us much about humility in the months to come and more than we ever wanted to know about modern warfare.

What reports have you heard in Babylon about the military operations in Jerusalem?

JEREMIAH with Baruch

First month
10th year in the reign
of King Zedekiah

Dear Uncle Shallum,

It looks as though the Babylonian army will not mount a full-scale attack as yet. They have surrounded Jerusalem with encampments and battle stations in order to cut off contact between ourselves and our allies outside the city walls. The blockade accomplishes another purpose as well: it prevents our bringing goods into the city, even crops from our own fields. For now, the city storehouses are well-stocked, but we know this forced isolation will cause some trouble for us in the days ahead.

King Nebuchadnezzar has shown once again that he is a patient man, content to wait many months if necessary for a victory of which he is certain. Whether the people of Jerusalem surrender from fright or from hunger is a matter of indifference to him, or even if they should be slaughtered to the last man, woman, and child. I suspect a great deal of suffering could be averted, if only our leaders would recognize that defeat is inevitable and quick surrender is our best option.

Now that farm fields and pastures are inaccessible to the Hebrew people, I wonder whether they will continue to practice pagan fertility rituals. What possible benefit could they expect when they have been cut off from the land which supplies their food? Will they find new ways to follow their animal instincts and satisfy their lust? Or will they finally acknowledge the true source of all their blessings? You can be sure, Uncle, I will take the opportunity to remind them of the bountiful goodness and mercy of the Lord.

It will be more difficult from now on to send letters into and out of Jerusalem. My friend, the soldier Zerubbaz, says he can arrange it, but delivery will be unpredictable. In any event, please do not stop writing, because I need your counsel more than ever. It would be best to leave my name off the outside of your letters and simply address them to the quartermaster at the fourth encampment, where my friend is stationed.

Did I ever tell you what occurred after Zerubbaz was turned away from the temple? One of the temple officials tried to cause trouble for him by reporting him to his superiors. The official told a Babylonian captain stationed near the temple that Zerubbaz was friendly with prophets and priests. On hearing that, the captain, a big, burly man, burst out laughing. He said young fellows are entitled to their friends, even odd and silly old men who practice elaborate superstitions. Later, Zerubbaz and I were able to sneak into the temple at certain quiet times of the day to worship the Lord.

I have grown close to Zerubbaz in the months since he embraced the Hebrew faith, and I will miss my frequent contacts with him and other Babylonians I have come to know. They are not bad people but are compelled by circumstances to be our enemies. Now we are separated by city walls and by the stupidity of our leaders.

I must admit (with some chagrin) I am relieved that the Babylonian generals have finally taken action, though as yet they have only put up a blockade. Now I can hope that the people (some of them, anyway) will see I was right in warning them to repent and return to the Lord.

Let me know how many months it takes for this letter to reach you.
JEREMIAH
by the hand of Baruch

Third month
10th year Zedekiah

Diary entry:

The Babylonian army has retreated from Jerusalem! For five months they surrounded the city, preparing for battle and attacking anyone who tried to enter or leave. Then, last week, the Egyptian army made a surprise appearance. I suppose these visitors from the south hope to impress the Babylonians with their audacity and perhaps incite rebellion among the Hebrew leaders. Does anyone seriously believe the Egyptian army is a threat to Nebuchadnezzar? The Babylonian generals pulled back their troops, it is true, but anyone with eyes and ears can see that this retreat is temporary—the puny Egyptian army cannot hold off the powerful Babylonian forces for long.

Nevertheless, I quickly made plans to take advantage of the situation. I decided to venture outside the city walls to visit Anathoth, where I need to conduct business with some friends. Naturally I assumed that Baruch would go with me, but he outright refused. Damn him!

Baruch was more argumentative and stubborn than I've ever known him to be; he insisted that the trip was still too dangerous. Who does he think he is, a prophet? He's had aspirations in that direction for several years now, even after I told him this was no time for him to seek glory for himself.

The silly man thinks there is a greater honor in being called "prophet" than "scribe." How wrong he is! A prophet shouts into the wind and the words are blown away, but a scribe gives people something to catch hold of. The words he chooses to preserve in writing provide inspiration and guidance to many people for a long time to come.

Baruch has the skill, talent, and patience to be an excellent scribe. He works quietly and faithfully at his desk, where he accomplishes far more than he could do as a prophet, with all the notoriety *that* brings. And surely he must know that I depend on him utterly.

I told Baruch we must be content to be what the Lord made us, not strive to be something we are not. He seemed offended by this statement and sulked about for a bit. But prophecy is difficult and dangerous work. In this evil time, I told Baruch, it is hard enough just to preserve life and limb while doing the work one is called to do. The Lord has assured me that Baruch's life will be spared, wherever he goes, yet he still refuses to go with me to Anathoth!

Baruch knew I was angry that he would not go with me, but still he would not change his mind. I'll go by myself, and when I return, he'll know that his fear of traveling outside the city was groundless.

Third month
10th year in the reign
of King Zedekiah

Dear Uncle,

Pharaoh has come to the rescue! A mighty army of squeaking Egyptian mice has frightened away the roaring multitude of Babylonian lions! I speak in jest, of course. It is true that the Egyptian army has marched into Judah and the Babylonian army has temporarily withdrawn, but I have no illusions that we are rescued. In fact, this "invasion" will accomplish nothing, and it may provoke a desire for revenge by our Babylonian foes.

Can you see the irony of the situation? Egyptian chariots tried to follow the Hebrew people out of Egypt once before, to take them back into slavery. Their malicious intent was frustrated by the flood waters of the Red Sea, and the Hebrew people were delivered to safety. Now the bumbling fools from the south have finally found their way to Judah, intending to save the Hebrews, and what will be the result? Destruction! When they want to do us harm, they help us; when they want to help us, they do us harm!

King Zedekiah is giddy with anticipation; he believes the Egyptian army will be his salvation. Yesterday he sent another delegation of courtiers to ask me to pray for him and seek the Lord's favor. I prayed, and the word of the Lord came to me.

I told the courtiers to tell their king that Pharaoh's army would go back to Egypt. The Chaldeans will immediately return and resume their siege until they have brought Jerusalem to its knees. Even if the Chaldean army were defeated and only a few wounded men survived, those few would rise up and burn the city down.

Do you think the king will listen? Neither the king, nor his servants, nor the people of the land will listen; they prefer to deceive themselves. Therefore, this people will suffer and die for their folly.

While the blockade is lifted, I will make a short excursion to see friends in Anathoth. I would rather not make the trip alone, but if I must, I will. I have tried to convince Baruch to go with me, but he hesitates to leave Jerusalem. What is he afraid of? I have told him to his face that I suspect laziness, as much as prudence, prevents his traveling. He taxes my patience sometimes.

Everything is unsettled in Jerusalem, even the weather. We hear distant thunder, yet it will not rain.

J. with Baruch

Sixth month
10th year in the reign
of King Zedekiah

Dear Uncle,

For the last two weeks, I have been in prison at the court of the guard. You need not worry about me, though, because the guards here treat me well. I am given a loaf of bread each day from the bakers' street, and Baruch is allowed to attend to my other needs. He is also able to write letters for me, which had been forbidden at the other place.

You see, before coming here, I was imprisoned in a dungeon at the house of Jonathan the secretary. Conditions there were much worse. I was beaten and barely fed for many weeks. But luckily the king summoned me to his palace to ask if there had been any word from the Lord Yahweh. I told the truth, that he, the king, would be delivered into the hand of the king of Babylon. After giving him that cheerful news, I asked him please not to send me back to the house of Jonathan the secretary, where I might die. King Zedekiah, who still wishes to preserve my life in case I should be useful to him, gave orders that I be turned over to the court of the guard, so here I am.

You may ask, why did they put me in prison in the first place? Let me go backward in time and tell you all that has taken place since I last wrote you.

About eight months ago, you recall, the Chaldean army came against Jerusalem and besieged it, just as I had predicted. They were not able to take the city immediately, but they set up a blockade to cut off communication between the city and the countryside, and they cut off deliveries of food. We had set aside reserve supplies, of course, but we knew they could not last forever.

The word of the Lord came to me, telling me there was still time for King Zedekiah to save his own life and the lives of his people, provided he surrender to the Chaldean army. If he did so, he would be taken captive and carried away to Babylon, where he would die in peace with all due honors and laments. Unfortunately, the king would not listen, and I was compelled to give him a crueler message, a prediction of his own downfall. This much I had already told you.

To make things worse, King Zedekiah established a covenant with Yahweh and the people, and then promptly broke it. While we were under siege and people were beginning to see the necessity of hiding away food for their families, the king made a pact with the princes and the people to set free all Hebrew slaves. He published an official edict, declaring that no Jew should enslave another Jew. The Lord must have been pleased when the people obeyed the edict and freed their slaves.

A joyful shout went up from Jerusalem; even under such dire conditions, the slaves rejoiced to be free. Many were already hungry, and their masters who sent them on their way gave them no share of the provisions which remained. The freed men were obliged to do the most menial jobs in exchange for a bit of bread.

Before long, a young female slave named Miriam appeared at my door, asking to be joined to my household. She said I had been kind to her once when I visited her master's house. It must have been many years ago, because I did not remember ever having seen her. I explained to her that my servants and I had very little to eat, but she pleaded to stay. She said starvation in my household was better than the life she had known as a slave. How could I refuse?

But this state of affairs did not last long. As I mentioned in the last letter I wrote, Pharaoh's army came marching up from the south, jangling their armor. The Chaldean troops, fearing a quick attack for which they were not prepared, pulled back into the hills. As soon as the fields around Jerusalem were left unguarded, the princes and the people decided to take back their slaves and rule over them again. They wasted no time in sending the slaves out into the fields to harvest whatever half-grown food crops they could find.

Miriam's master came to my house, with his sons, and demanded that she be turned over to him. I protested, to no avail. They entered my house and dragged the poor girl away. Her wailing, like that of a child who has lost its mother, remains in my ears to this day. These Hebrew people are jackals, preying on the helpless and stealing what does not belong to them. Tell me, Uncle, is there any hope for them? I think not.

The Lord Yahweh spoke to me again. He told me that the Chaldean army would return and lay waste to Jerusalem. He said that because the Hebrew people took back their slaves and did not loosen their bonds as he commanded, he would let loose warfare, plague, and starvation everywhere. The leaders and all the people will be captured and killed, their dead bodies left in fields and highways to be eaten by vultures. The cities of Judah will be demolished. By speaking like this, I made many new enemies among the princes and the people.

Now, Uncle, I can explain to you why I was put in prison. While the Chaldean army was out of the way, I had hoped to make a quick trip to Anathoth to settle some affairs with friends. As I was leaving Jerusalem through the Benjamin Gate, a sentry stopped me and accused me of deserting to the Chaldeans. I denied this falsehood, but he did not believe me. The man turned me over to some of my new enemies, the hostile princes, who gave me a beating and locked me up in the dungeon under the house of Jonathan the secretary. So now you know, Uncle, how I came to be put in prison. (It pains me to admit that Baruch tried to warn me of the danger in leaving Jerusalem, but I ignored his wise counsel.)

We in Jerusalem await the inexorable judgment of Yahweh.

Your nephew JEREMIAH
by the hand of Baruch

Tenth month
10th year in the reign
of King Zedekiah

Dear Uncle,

I am still shut up at the court of the guard. The jailers are not unkind to me, and anyway they are too weak to exert themselves very much. Hunger has consumed us all, rich and poor, young and old, prisoner and guard.

As I predicted, the Chaldean army has returned, the Egyptians have retreated, and we are once again prevented from bringing provisions into the city. Our food supplies have dwindled to nearly nothing. The daily ration of bread has gone from one loaf to half-a-loaf to a small piece no bigger than my fist. I have seen children gnawing on leaves and stems plucked from fig trees to relieve their aching stomachs.

Yet in the midst of such distress, the Lord told me of a happy event that would soon come about. He said your son would visit me in the court of the guard, with an offer I could not turn down. Sure enough, Hanamel my cousin came the next day and said to me, "You are my closest relative and therefore, in accordance with the law, I am offering you the option to buy my land. Come, buy the field in your native town of Anathoth in the region of Benjamin." So I did!

The Jews who were sitting in the court of the guard gathered around to watch; they were glad to see anything that would divert their attention from the privation and suffering which afflict everyone. First I weighed out seventeen shekels of silver on the scales and gave the money to my cousin. Then I signed the deed spelling out the details of the purchase and sealed it in the presence of witnesses. I gave both the sealed copy and an open copy to Baruch and asked him to preserve them in a pottery jug, as is the custom.

This little transaction showed me possibilities for the future I could not otherwise have imagined. Buying the field gave me hope that buying and selling of houses and farmlands would one day be resumed. The Lord would indeed restore the fortunes of his people.

Then I prayed to the Lord in the presence of Hanamel and Baruch and all the witnesses who had gathered round. I praised the Lord, saying it was he who created the earth and who continues to pour out loving kindness on his people. He rewards and punishes, judging each man with perfect justice. Long ago he brought his people Israel out of Egypt with many miracles, and he gave them the land promised to their fathers, a land flowing with milk and honey. All this I prayed in the presence of those assembled in the court of the guard.

The purchase was such a happy event and a hopeful sign that I did not wish to disclose the word of the Lord which came to me a short time later.

Behold, I am the Lord, the God of all flesh; is anything too hard for me? Therefore, thus says the Lord: Behold, I am giving this city into the hands of the Chaldeans and into the hand of Nebuchadnezzar king of Babylon, and he shall take it. The Chaldeans who are fighting against this city shall come and set this city on fire, and burn it, with the houses on whose roofs incense has been offered to Baal and drink offerings have been poured out to other gods, to provoke me to anger. For the sons of Israel and the sons of Judah have done nothing but evil in my sight from their youth; the sons of Israel have done nothing but provoke me to anger by the work of their hands, says the Lord.

In spite of this unhappy prophecy, I remain hopeful, Uncle, because the Lord assured me he would bring upon this people the blessings he promised them. The first gift he gives them will be a sense of fearful awe, to keep them faithful to him. He will make a new covenant with them, one which will never end, and he will firmly establish their roots in this place. The Lord told me yet again that farmlands will be bought and sold in Judah, as we did today with the field in Anathoth.

Ever since Hanamel went away, I have been wondering what he would do with the money I paid him. It had been lying untouched in my leather purse for months; there is so little left in Jerusalem that is worth buying. Could he have heard of some hidden food supplies? If so, he will pay a high price for them!

It was good to see my cousin again. Let me assure you that he and his family are getting along as well as anyone. He is the same Hanamel I knew as a boy: slow of speech and sleepy-looking, but sharp as a needle.

My love to you,

JEREMIAH by the hand of Baruch

Twelfth month
10th year in the reign
of King Zedekiah

Dear Uncle,

The situation here has grown worse. Since my last letter to you, no land transactions or other happy events have occurred to lighten the monotony or the misery of the people confined within the walls of Jerusalem. There is no food for sale anywhere; all that remains is what people have hidden away for themselves. Whenever a secret cache of food is discovered, word travels quickly to the surrounding streets, and soon a listless but relentless crowd pushes its way to the food supply and devours it like an army of hungry ants. The hungry people do not respect property or position—I believe they would break into the king's palace if guards did not wield spears at every gate.

I cannot condemn people who steal food when they are starving. Yet there have been rumors of much more horrible crimes. I will not even pronounce the names of these crimes, or ask Baruch to write them, but I will ask him to transcribe the prophecy which the Lord spoke to me in his wrath:

Even the jackals give the breast and suckle their young,
 but the daughter of my people has become cruel,
 like the ostriches in the wilderness.
The tongue of the nursling cleaves to the roof of its mouth for thirst;
 the children beg for food, but no one gives to them.
Those who feasted on dainties perish in the streets;
 those who were brought up in purple lie on ash heaps.
Happier were the victims of the sword than the victims of hunger,
 who pined away, stricken by want of the fruits of the field.
The hands of compassionate women have boiled their own children;
 they became their food in the destruction of the daughter of my people.
Cry aloud to the Lord! O daughter of Zion!
Let tears stream down like a torrent day and night!
Give yourself no rest, your eyes no respite!
Arise, cry out in the night, at the beginning of the watches!
Pour out your heart like water before the presence of the Lord!
Lift your hands to him for the lives of your children,
 who faint for hunger at the head of every street.
Look, O Lord, and see! With whom hast thou dealt thus?
Should women eat their offspring, the children of their tender care?
Should priest and prophet be slain in the sanctuary of the Lord?

If, in fact, the people have advanced so far in their depravity, then all my preaching is in vain. If they are already walking the path toward condemnation and destruction, what good can I do? Should I simply turn away and leave them to their fate? It seems as if the sin of Judah is written indelibly on their hearts, etched sharply and deeply with a diamond-tipped pen.

So you see, Uncle, I am weary of the hunger, fear, confinement, and restlessness that we all suffer in Jerusalem, but more than that, I am weary of the seeming futility of my work. Nevertheless, I feel sure that something is going to change. Whether for good or evil, our situation here will soon be essentially altered.

I hope to have better news for you in my next letter.
JEREMIAH
with Baruch

First month
11th year in the reign
of King Zedekiah

Dear Uncle,

The king has demonstrated once more that he has no backbone. A few days ago some of the princes heard me say again, as I have said many times before, that the people who stay in this city shall die, but those who go out and surrender to the Chaldeans shall live. The princes angrily accused me of betraying the people and undermining the soldiers who remain in the city. They petitioned King Zedekiah for the right to execute me.

Without considering whether I spoke the truth, the king put me in their hands and claimed he could do nothing to protect me. Humbug! He's a spineless coward.

These arrangements with the king I found out about later. For me, the first indication that anything was wrong came one night when I was awakened by loud voices in my cell. Someone kicked me in the stomach as I lay on my pallet, still sleepy and disoriented. A couple of large men grabbed my arms and jerked me up to a standing position, maintaining their tight grip as they hustled me outside into the courtyard. Then the royal ruffians engaged in a brief debate as to how they should dispose of me. The princes did not have the courage to slay me outright, but they threw me into a deep, muddy pit located in the court of the guard. Fortunately there was no water in the pit, or I might have drowned. Instead, I sank slowly into the stinking mire. How long I could have survived there I don't know, probably not more than a couple of days.

My rescue was carried out by a most unlikely character. It happened while I lay in a stupor, with my body curled up in the damp slime on the bottom of the cistern and my head propped against the hard earthen wall. My hands and feet were already numb with cold, and I was beginning to feel faint from hunger.

I was brought to my senses by a squeaky voice calling my name from far above. When I looked up, I could see nothing but dark silhouettes framing a small, bright patch of light. The squeaky voice told me they were going to pull me out, if I would do what they said.

Naturally it occurred to me that these people might want to kill me quickly instead of leaving me to starve, but I could hardly question them from where I sat; in fact, I could barely see or hear them. I decided to cooperate.

Some old rags and clothes came dangling down to me on a rope, and the voice told me to put them under my armpits. I tied the rope around my chest and called up toward the patch of light. Then they pulled me up.

You can imagine how I looked and smelled after sitting in the mire for almost a day and night, perhaps even worse than when I fell into the sheep stall as a boy. Do you remember? If this happens again, the city officials will ask me to pose as a figurehead on the Dung Gate!

When I came out, I found myself face-to-face with a small black man whose soft gentle eyes revealed goodness and compassion. Actually his skin was not quite black, but darker than any Egyptian I have known. I recognized him to be Ebed-melech, an Ethiopian eunuch who lives in the king's house. He felt sorry for me and knew I had committed no crime deserving death, so he convinced the king to allow my rescue.

Thanks to Ebed-melech, I have once again escaped serious injury or death. The only noticeable aftereffects are some bruises on my buttocks from bouncing off the walls of the cistern.

Though I barely knew Ebed-melech before this incident, I now consider him to be a friend. Yesterday the word of the Lord came to me concerning Ebed-melech: "On the day this city is attacked, he will not fall by the sword or be handed over to his enemies but will be delivered to safety, because he put his trust in the Lord." My new friend will be glad to hear these words, don't you think?

JEREMIAH with Baruch

Second month
11th year in the reign
of King Zedekiah

Dear Uncle,

Strange as it may seem, I still have some slight hope that King Zedekiah may yet turn to the Lord and do what is right. Though he has disappointed me often, I continue to regard him (most of the time) with affection. Could I be deceiving myself? Am I clinging to an ideal image of the man, borne out of the optimism we all felt when he first came to power, after the reign of his evil brother Jehoiakim? Tell me what you think.

The king sent for me yesterday. He obviously wanted our meeting to be kept secret, for we met in the third entrance of the temple, where his courtiers would never find us. He asked me to be completely honest and forthright in answering his questions. Have I ever done otherwise?

Still, I answered with some caution: "If I tell the truth, will you not have me put to death? If I give advice, will you not ignore it?" The king swore by the Lord Yahweh that he would not have me killed.

So I told him for the twentieth time that if he would only surrender to the king of Babylon, then he and all his children would survive and Jerusalem would still stand. But if he refused to surrender, then the Chaldeans will incinerate the city. Furthermore, he himself will be captured and punished.

King Zedekiah's face turned ashen, his eyes narrowed, and his expression hardened as he listened to my words. With clenched teeth he answered, saying he was afraid he might fall into the hands of Jews who had already gone over to the Chaldeans and they might threaten his life. I assured him this would not happen.

Then I told him of a vision shown me by the Lord: All the women in the king's house were forcefully taken out and handed over to the young Babylonian princes. As the women were led away they spoke these words to King Zedekiah:

"Your trusted friends have deceived you and prevailed against you;
now that your feet are sunk in the mire, they turn away from you."

Then I said that all the rest of his household, including his sons and even the king himself, would be taken captive and handled roughly by the Chaldeans.

King Zedekiah twitched nervously before responding. He told me that as much as he feared the power and authority of the Babylonians, he was more afraid of his own people, especially his royal allies in the court who had shown absolute ruthlessness in grasping for power. He was sure they would kill him in an instant if he displeased them in any way.

The king was trembling as if a cold wind had blown hard against his naked body. I put my hands on his shoulders to steady him and told him he must have courage to take the right course of action, regardless of the consequences to himself. He looked at me with the expression of a frightened dog that runs away with its tail between its legs. As tears came to his eyes, he turned away from me and muttered, "I can't, I can't." I quietly recited three psalms while he stood sobbing with his back to me, and then I waited a few minutes more for him to regain his composure.

At last King Zedekiah turned to face me, his eyes swollen and teeth bared. His stained and missing teeth made his mouth look like a dark hole cut from a patch of pasty white skin. I felt a swell of pity for him.

Assuming a bold tone, the king said I must promise to tell no one of this conversation. He told me to say to the princes, if they should ask about our meeting, that I was begging the king not to send me back to the dungeon under the house of Jonathan the secretary. The princes did ask, and I answered just as the king had instructed.

Now I am back in the court of the guard, still alive, but hungry and tired like the rest of the people in Jerusalem.

Unhappily, I think that King Zedekiah will once again ignore the word of the Lord; he will not surrender to the Babylonians (as he must do ultimately in the face of their overwhelming strength) but will continue to annoy them with flea bites.

What shall I do? Has the time come to condemn Zedekiah to his horrible fate at the hands of the Babylonians, or perhaps the Jews? Am I to give up hope that this king will ever lead his people in the way of the Lord?

Or should I keep trying to change him, to persuade him to choose the right path? Zedekiah has been my friend for many years (since boyhood), and even my protector on occasion. How can I turn away from him?

I can hear you now, Uncle, telling me to trust in the Lord with all my heart. I am attempting to do that, while, at the same time, I earnestly await your advice.

JEREMIAH
by Baruch

Fourth month
11th year Zedekiah

Dairy entry:

Panic has overtaken the city. The Chaldean army is making preparations for a massive assault, after months of encampment outside the city walls. We hear daily reports of siege mounds and battering rams made ready and horsemen and archers preparing to attack. The army is so close we can almost hear the snorting and neighing of their horses.

The people in the city are weak and dispirited from lack of food and water, yet the terror in their hearts has given them new energy. The ground seems to quake as so many frightened feet run back and forth with nowhere to go. They dare not flee the city because they can see long lines of warriors on every side. Their choice is to be slain outside the city walls or to stay and drink the poisoned water of defeat and dishonor.

We have sinned against the Lord, and he has sent us serpents who bite. What is left for us to do but weep?

Thus says the Lord of hosts:
"Consider, and call for the mourning women to come;
 send for the skillful women to come;
 let them make haste and raise a wailing over us,
 that our eyes may run down with tears,
 and our eyelids gush with water.
For a sound of wailing is heard from Zion:
 'How we are ruined!
 We are utterly shamed, because we have left the land,
 because they have cast down our dwellings.'"
Hear, O women, the word of the Lord,
 and let your ear receive the word of his mouth;
 teach to your daughters a lament, and each to her neighbor a dirge.
For death has come up into our windows, it has entered our palaces,
 cutting off children from the streets
 and the young men from the squares.
Speak, "Thus says the Lord:
 'The dead bodies of men shall fall like dung upon the open field,
 like sheaves after the reaper, and none shall gather them.'"

Fourth month
11th year in the reign
of King Zedekiah

Dear Uncle,

The battle for Jerusalem has begun. Baruch and I do our best to stay out of the way, but we cannot avoid hearing the clash of weapons and the anguished cries of people who are injured or compelled to watch their loved ones suffer.

According to what we can gather from the frightened souls around us, the first breach of the city wall occurred at the Ephraim Gate on the north side of the city. The Chaldeans constructed siegeworks near the gate by which to scale the wall. A few of their men succeeded in getting to the top; from there they rained down arrows and spears on the Hebrew soldiers stationed just inside the wall. Meanwhile, a battering ram was applied again and again to the gate until it began to crack. When they had once breached the wall, panic broke out among the people, and it became easier for the Chaldeans to break down gates all around the city. Now the Chaldean army units advance into the streets one after another, like waves from the sea.

I think the fighting cannot continue much longer, because the Hebrew soldiers are weak from malnourishment and their weapons are inferior. Many are reduced to throwing rocks when their supply of spears and arrows is exhausted. In hand-to-hand combat, their daggers and clubs are ineffectual against Babylonian soldiers equipped with helmets, shields, and coats of armor. I understand also that communication with our allies in other cities is completely cut off.

A rumor is flying about that King Zedekiah has taken his guards and fled, leaving the city at night by the king's garden and making his way east toward the Arabah. We have also heard that Nergal-sharezer and some of the other Babylonian princes are so confident of victory that they came and sat in the middle gate as if they were presiding over a new government of occupation.

I believe that Yahweh will finally bring to fulfillment the prophecy concerning Jerusalem:

> *All who pass along the way clap their hands at you;*
> > *they hiss and wag their heads at the daughter of Jerusalem;*
> > *"Is this the city which was called the perfection of beauty,*
> > *the joy of all the earth?"*
> *All your enemies rail against you;*
> > *they hiss, they gnash their teeth, they cry: "We have destroyed her!*
> > *Ah, this is the day we longed for; now we have it; we see it!"*
> *The Lord has done what he purposed, has carried out his threat;*
> > *as he ordained long ago, he has demolished without pity;*
> > *he has made the enemy rejoice over you,*
> > *and exalted the might of your foes.*

When I consider the glorious reign of King David and the grandeur of King Solomon, my soul weeps for this once-proud people, because I know the beautiful hills will soon be brought low and Mount Zion will be humbled.

As we look in horror at what is happening around us, Baruch and I find comfort in psalms and prayers. We have recited together many times the words of King David:

> *I trust in thee, O Lord, I say, "Thou art my God."*
> *My times are in thy hand;*
> > *deliver me from the hand of my enemies and persecutors!*
> *Let thy face shine on thy servant;*
> > *save me in thy steadfast love!*

It is not much in the way of reassurance to tell you that so far we have been able to keep calm in the midst of panic.

We know that you and the other exiles want as much information as we can provide about the siege of Jerusalem. I am sorry there is no good news, but perhaps the worst will soon be over. I will write as often as I can.

JEREMIAH by Baruch

Fifth month
11th year in the reign
of King Zedekiah

Uncle,

I dictate in haste, in the midst of devastation. Since my last letter, the army of Nebuchadnezzar has overrun the city; they will soon demolish it. Many are dead, and most of the people still alive are in chains. Only the old and the weak are allowed to roam the streets freely.

I set out this morning, intending to pray at the temple, but I never made it that far. As I entered the main street, my stomach heaved at what I saw. Bodies were lying in ghastly poses, sometimes piled in a heap where an entire family had been butchered while they were trying to protect one another. I vomited until there was nothing left to bring up, and still my stomach retched.

I returned home only an hour ago. My feet are soaked with blood, up to the ankles, and my face is wet with tears. When I see the sorrows of the people, I give thanks to Yahweh that he commanded me not to marry. Those with families suffer double and triple sorrows.

Apart from this, I have heard horrible rumors about the fate of the king. When I know the truth about him, I will write to you again. These sad tidings are enough for one letter, which I send in the hand of Shazban, a soldier who has lately befriended me. He is the messenger for Nebuzaradan, the captain of the guard, so I am confident my letters will be carried to Babylon immediately, with the military dispatches. You may, if you wish, send a return letter with him.

I have not heard anything from Zerubbaz in three weeks, and I am worried about him. Pray for us, Uncle.

J. by Baruch

Sixth month
11th year Zedekiah

Diary entry:

I am so weary that my head feels as useless as a heavy stone set upon my shoulders. My mind is confused and I can't think clearly. This dullness of mind makes it difficult for me to find the words to describe what I have seen—I have sat here stupidly for nearly an hour and made barely a mark with my pen.

For many days I've had no restful sleep. Horrible, vivid dreams fill my troubled nights so that I wake suddenly and see before me all that I have witnessed in the last month.

It must have been ten days ago that Baruch told me he had seen Mara's husband, the scoundrel Zaccai, running in the street with a bundle on his back. Baruch followed him as far as he could, until his sore old knees prevented his going any farther; he told me Zaccai appeared to be headed for the Fountain Gate on the south side of the city. Zaccai ran like a scared rat, Baruch said, stopping now and then to catch his breath and look around furtively to see if anyone was observing him. I knew right away that the scoundrel had deserted his family in hopes of escaping to the hills and saving his own skin.

My first thought was for Mara and her children. I went to her house immediately, but it was empty. I ran around the streets and nearby houses, searching everywhere, but found no trace of the family. Finally, in utter exhaustion, I returned home.

The next morning, Baruch offered to go with me to continue the search. We began at Mara's house and made our way north toward the temple, through the confusion of this besieged city. We passed one house where the inhabitants had shut themselves in with barricades and were still resisting the Chaldean soldiers who were attempting to storm the house. The soldiers ignored us as we passed by—what harm could they fear from two unarmed old men?

We stepped over a pile of dead bodies blocking the street and were nauseated by the stench. Sitting in the clotted dirt beside the bodies, we saw a withered old woman dressed in sackcloth, silently picking up handfuls of dry dust and dropping it on her bare head. Nearby, a young woman was grinding her forehead into the dirt. Infants and young children lay whimpering along the way, too weak to cry aloud for their dead mothers.

Baruch and I kept walking, glancing at bodies, both dead and alive, hoping to recognize a face. I saw a small group of people at the end of an alley and made my way toward them, an awful premonition swelling in my chest as I approached. I recognized Mara, the woman I love, lying with her little son in her arms and her two daughters nestled close, one on each side. I fell to my knees and looked into her beautiful hazel eyes, and I took her hand in mine. I told her that I loved her with all my heart and that I had loved her since the moment I first saw her. I raised her cold hand to my face as tears streamed down my cheeks. She looked at me with eyes wide open and unblinking, full of understanding, and a peaceful expression on her face.

I didn't hear Baruch walk up behind me. He knelt beside me and touched my shoulder. He pried my hands open and gently laid Mara's hand back on her lap. Then he led me away.

I can't remember what happened after that. I suppose Baruch took me home. My eyes are burning and my throat is parched. My head is clouded and confused with the events that have overtaken the city, and I cannot think clearly.

Seventh month
11th year in the reign
of King Zedekiah

Dear Uncle,

I send you more sad tidings from the place that was Jerusalem.

We suffer unending misery. The city is destroyed. Fires smolder in every quarter, and a thick cloud of smoke hangs over everything. Many of the people have been killed or carried away in chains. For those of us left behind, food is so scarce we eat rats off the street. I fear pestilence and plague, the daughters of famine.

One of those captured (I have heard it confirmed by Chaldean soldiers) was the king himself, along with all his sons. It is a terrible fate that has befallen King Zedekiah, more terrible than death.

It is said that Zedekiah, his sons, and his bodyguards fled the city late one night after the invasion began. The Chaldean army set out in pursuit and captured them in the plains of Jericho. They bound them and carried them north to Riblah, where Nebuchadnezzar king of Babylon issued his verdict.

At Nebuchadnezzar's command, the Chaldeans slaughtered King Zedekiah's sons before his very eyes. He will see nothing else; only that unspeakable horror will he see forever in his mind's eye, for they put out his eyes after they slew his sons.

To heap indignities upon the king's family, they left his sons' bodies to rot or to be eaten by wild beasts and birds. The miserable old man was carried away in chains to Babylon, to live out his days in prison.

Why has Yahweh imposed this punishment upon the king? Were his sins greater than those of Jehoiakim, his brother, who would not listen to the words of Yahweh? King Zedekiah listened and sometimes wanted to obey, but in the end he chose to disobey; now he has surely been punished to the utmost.

Sitting amidst the ruins, I have been pondering why it was that Zedekiah failed to fulfill our high hopes and expectations. Having observed his father and his brother who were kings before him, he ought to have learned how to lead and govern.

His father Josiah brought justice and righteousness to the land by seeking the Lord and showing loyalty to him. Josiah's reforms, while not perfect in their execution, sought to renew the covenant between Yahweh and his people; the Hebrew people drew closer to the Lord than they had done in many years.

On the other hand, Zedekiah's brother Jehoiakim led the people astray. He allowed them to worship graven images and false idols and to disregard the laws of Moses, and he persistently did what was evil in the sight of the Lord. The people followed him and their punishment was swift.

Why did Zedekiah not learn the lesson of his father and his brother? He could see what was right, but he chose to ignore it. The wicked king Jehoiakim had no vision to begin with, but Zedekiah, through cowardice and indecision, willingly obscured his own vision.

Two years ago, he went whoring after Egypt, thinking the Egyptians could turn back the mighty army of Babylon, a task as difficult as holding back the rising tide. Furthermore, Zedekiah engaged in harlotry with carved wooden idols, the false gods of other nations, and he persistently listened to lying prophets. By his unfaithfulness to the Lord, the king brought justice on himself: he acted as if he were blind, and now he *is* blind. May Yahweh have mercy on him as he lives and dies.

While I am speaking of kings, I am compelled to say a few words to you about Nebuchadnezzar. He is no worshipper of Yahweh, yet he is nevertheless a servant of Yahweh, for he is carrying out the Lord's purpose. He has conquered Jerusalem and punished the people. As long as he continues to do his duty honorably as a soldier and a king, Nebuchadnezzar will continue to be a servant of Yahweh. But if he strays outside the bounds of human decency and does what he has not been called to do (as I begin to suspect he has already done), then the wrath of the Lord will descend upon him as well.

Can things get any worse for the people of Israel? Let us hope not.
JEREMIAH and Baruch

New Hope

Second month
1st year in the
governorship of Gedeliah

Dear Uncle,

I hesitate to tell you this, but I could have come to you. The captain of the guard, Nebuzaradan, offered me safe passage to Babylon, which I declined. Can you forgive me? I know that you have no family members to tend to your needs since Orpah died, and that my being there would be a comfort to you in your old age. But I also know that Yahweh intends for me to stay with the poor, miserable souls who remain in Judah.

Here is an account of how things stand: The fighting has stopped, the people have accepted defeat, and the land is quiet once again. It is a different sort of quiet that prevails now in Judah, eerie and hollow and devoid of optimism. Hunger and disease lurk about, but what has affected the people most is fear—morbid fear of unknown tribulations which lie ahead.

The Babylonians have carried into exile many more of our people, some who surrendered before the final siege, as well as most of those who were left in the city after its destruction. Some of your old friends are among the captives; they are now following the same path you did some eleven or twelve years ago, slowly making their way over mountains and plateaus, across valleys and rivers, heading toward the great city of Babylon. Do you recall how long it took to travel from Jerusalem to Babylon? This group will move more slowly than you did, I think, since more women, children, and older people are included among them.

The recent deportation was ordered by Nebuzaradan, the captain of the guard. The only people he allowed to remain in Judah are the poorest folks, who own nothing; but even as he planned the mass exodus of the Hebrew people to Babylon, Nebuzaradan saw to it that the poor people left behind were given vineyards and fields to cultivate.

I was sorry to see so many of my people depart, knowing that some will die on the journey and the remainder will live in exile for so long that I shall never see them again. On the other hand, Jerusalem is destroyed and there is no place here for them to stay; and besides, the people who go to Babylon may renew their faith in the Lord, once they are removed from the corruption which has infected the religious establishment here in

Judah. You will encourage them, I am confident, to worship Yahweh and to listen to the voice of Ezekiel and the other true prophets who went with you into exile.

Now I must tell you, Uncle, about the events which led to my decision to remain in Judah. Some time after the battle had ended, a battalion of Chaldean soldiers marched through the streets of Jerusalem, shouting for all Hebrews to come out of their hiding places. When they found us, they pushed us into a line and clamped chains around our wrists and necks; after they had gathered a sufficient number, they forced us all, young and old, strong and weak, to move quickly to a holding area just outside the city wall. The strongest captives did their best to support and assist the weaker ones who were linked to them by heavy chains.

Baruch and I made an effort to keep within sight of one another. We waited for hours in the holding area, along with hundreds of others. Children cried out occasionally, but for the most part, people were too hungry, weary, and dispirited to speak or weep. A few old women were allowed to carry water jugs to those who were thirsty, but otherwise we were offered no refreshment.

Finally, as the sun was reaching its highest point, we were told to arise and start walking. We plodded northward on the road to Anathoth. It was an odd feeling for me, to be heading toward my home with all the living bodies of Jerusalem chained to my body. But we did not stop in Anathoth. We proceeded north to Ramah, arriving considerably after dark. At last we were given something to eat, a bit of bread and some dried fruits. The chains were removed from our necks but not from our hands.

We surmised that all the survivors were to be gathered together in Ramah, in preparation for the long journey to Babylon. One of the Babylonian officers must have recognized me, because Baruch and I were soon separated from the other captives. We were given generous helpings of food and treated with more respect than we had been earlier. We guessed that the Babylonians were treating us well because they hoped Baruch and I would assist them in some way, perhaps by persuading the other prisoners to be cooperative. At any rate, our supposition was wrong, for our captors never asked us to do anything.

After three or four days, a couple of soldiers escorted us to a large tent. Inside the tent, surrounded by heavily armed soldiers but wearing no armor himself, sat Nebuzaradan, the captain of the guard. He politely asked us to sit, and then he proceeded to preach a sermon!

Nebuzaradan told us that our Lord Yahweh had carried out his promise to punish the people of Judah because they sinned against him. He said their disobedience demanded punishment. Baruch and I listened in amazement.

Then the captain of the guard surprised us again—he offered to release us! He ordered that the chains be removed right away from our wrists, and he gave us a choice: If we wished to go with the other captives to Babylon, he would see that we were well taken care of. But if we preferred to stay behind in Judah, he said that was all right too. After a short pause, he told us that if we stayed, he would place us under the protection of Gedeliah, whom King Nebuchadnezzar had recently appointed governor of the cities of Judah. Do you remember Gedeliah, the son of my old friend Ahikam and the grandson of Shaphan? He's a good fellow, from a good family.

We were offered food and drink in the tent of Nebuzaradan. While the captain watched us eat, Baruch and I considered the choice before us. We thought of our loved ones already residing in Babylon and those who would soon be joining them. We discussed the hazards of a long journey measured against the dangers for a conquered and unarmed people living in the midst of their enemies. We wondered how we would find food to survive if we stayed behind in Judah. It was not an easy decision to make, but we are now both firmly convinced that it is right for us to stay in this land which was promised to our fathers. I hope you understand that we are following the commands of Yahweh, but not following our hearts.

Once we made our decision to stay, Nebuzaradan gave us an allowance of food and a gift of Babylonian money, and he let us go. We went immediately to Mizpah, a city northwest of Ramah, where we found Gedeliah and his newly assembled court. Some refugees who had escaped from Jerusalem during the final battle had also made their way to Mizpah, as did some people who had been hiding for many months in the hills and the open country.

The people here are nervous about what will happen to them. There is some uncertainty, to be sure, but you need not worry, Uncle; I believe all of us are safe as long as we remain under the protection of Gedeliah. Indeed, I am allowing myself to hope this will be a new beginning for the people of Judah. I will write soon and let you know how things develop.

Please keep me informed about the newest exiles, once they arrive. Let me know who survived the journey, and how they are adjusting to captivity.

Your loving nephew,
JEREMIAH with Baruch

Third month
1st year in the
governorship of Gedeliah

Dear Uncle,

About two weeks ago Baruch and I decided we would go back to Jerusalem to see what remains of the city. Meeting with no objection from the governor and seeing no reason to delay our mission, we departed Mizpah the next day. We were able to travel quickly since we had nothing to carry but our skins of water and some light provisions.

As we approached the city, the odor of death was pervasive; it was not the smell of rotting flesh but rather the lingering scent of charred buildings and bodies. The Babylonians had burned everything in sight, as they said they would.

We came first to a Chaldean encampment outside the city wall. By then, Baruch and I were famished, as we had had very little to eat during our journey. The soldiers eyed us curiously, and one of them ran off to find a companion who could speak with us in the Hebrew tongue. Imagine my delight when the soldier returned with my old friend Zerubbaz!

The other soldiers watched in amazement as Baruch and I embraced our Babylonian friend. We told him what had happened to us after the siege, how we had been driven like cattle to Ramah and then freed by Nebuzaradan. We also told him how hungry we were.

Zerubbaz gave orders to some of his fellow soldiers, who went off in different directions. Before long, a new odor reached our nostrils, the odor of succulent meat roasting on a wood fire. Many, many months had gone by since Baruch and I had tasted (or even smelled) anything so delicious, so naturally our mouths watered and our stomachs yearned in expectation. What a feast it was! Well-seasoned meat of a young goat, so tender that it fell off the bones, went down easily with breadcakes and the rich, dark wine the soldiers kept pouring into our cups. They laughed at us when we motioned again and again for more—I am afraid Baruch and I made gluttons of ourselves on this occasion. You know how enticing good food can be after a long period of privation!

After we rested from our gluttony, Baruch and I arose and declared that we were going to walk into the city. Zerubbaz tried to dissuade us, on the grounds that we would be in danger from rats and other vermin. I think he also worried that seeing the devastation would affect us in ways we could not anticipate. He was right.

Since he could not dissuade us, our young friend insisted on going with us to the temple mount. As we approached the sacred site, we could not believe what we saw, or rather did not see. There was nothing but a heap of ashes where the magnificent temple of Solomon had once stood. The courtyards, the high walls fronted by bronze pillars, the vestibule with its beautiful cyprus door leading into the main hall, and the inner chambers of cedar and olivewood finely carved and overlaid with gold had all disappeared, burnt to the ground or dismantled. The blood rushed from my head when I saw the vacant space, and I held Baruch's arm to steady myself. Zerubbaz did not speak but motioned for us to sit on his cloak, which he had spread on a large stone. As we gazed at the ashheap, I thought of the hours I had spent on this site, preaching and praying. I wondered what had become of the incense altar, the lampstands, and the other splendid vessels Nebuchadnezzar left in the house of the Lord after his first conquest. I pondered also the fate of the ark of the covenant of Yahweh and its contents, the holy relics from the exodus.

As I sat there, the word of the Lord came into my head:

The Lord has destroyed without mercy all the habitations of Jacob;
in his wrath he has broken down the strongholds
of the daughter of Judah;
he has brought down to the ground in dishonor
the kingdom and its rulers.
He has cut down in fierce anger all the might of Israel;
he has withdrawn from them his right hand
in the face of the enemy;
he has burned like a flaming fire in Jacob, consuming all around.
He has broken down his booth like that of a garden,
laid in ruins the place of his appointed feasts;
the Lord has brought to an end in Zion
appointed feast and sabbath,
and in his fierce indignation has spurned king and priest.

Now we are back in Mizpah, and I have had time to reflect on the destruction of the temple. It was inevitable. Just as the house of worship in Shiloh was destroyed when the people did not listen to the Lord, so the temple in Jerusalem could not remain standing. But I am troubled still about losing the ark of the covenant. Can we continue to know with certainty that Yahweh is present with us if we have no tangible signs of his presence? Will the people feel that Yahweh has deserted them and left them alone in the world?

You have lived far away from the temple and the ark for many years, yet you have remained faithful to the Lord. Does he manifest himself to you in other ways? Can we hope for the same? Your wisdom is wanted here in Judah, for we are living in difficult times. Write soon.

JEREMIAH

with Baruch

Fifth month
1st year in the
governorship of Gedeliah

Dear Uncle,

We are still living in Mizpah. Our leader Gedeliah is a good and sensible man, a true worshipper of Yahweh. Word has gone out to all the nations that Nebuchadnezzar appointed Gedeliah governor of the Hebrew people left in Judah, the impoverished farmers and vinedressers who were not taken to Babylon.

Others besides these poor families have come to Mizpah to confer with Gedeliah. Ishmael, Johanan, and Seraiah, captains of those forces still roaming the open country, came to ask the new governor his intentions. Gedeliah told them they should not be afraid of the Chaldeans, but should serve the king of Babylon, and then all would be well with them. He offered to represent them before the king, if they would dwell in the land, plant crops, and harvest fruits and wine and oil. For the time being they seem inclined to do as he advises.

Jews in other lands have also heard that King Nebuchadnezzar left a remnant in Judah and appointed Gedeliah governor over them. People of Moab and Edom and Ammon are returning, a few at a time, from the places to which their families fled during the Babylonian assaults and the Assyrian invasion before that. Even more of our people will come as they learn what an excellent leader we have in Gedeliah.

Do you remember my telling you about the birth of Hanniel, son of Elasah, son of Shaphan? The boy is now ten years old, and for those ten years he has been the utter delight of his parents. He is a biddable child, willing to learn what his elders would teach him, which in his case has included a healthy dose of law and scripture. That is not unusual in a family such as his, but what is more surprising is that the child has shown remarkable ability to play musical instruments.

At the recent installation of the new governor Gedeliah (who, as you know, is first cousin to Hanniel), the boy played tunes on the lyre and psaltery to the great satisfaction of those in attendance. He also sang psalms with a voice I imagine to be as sweet and pure as King David's was. (You always told me that the psalms of David are music from heaven.) Those of us who attended will not soon forget the solemn ceremony and the lovely music; I was not the only person whose eyes were moist before it was over.

The word of the Lord came to me immediately afterwards:

"The people who survived the sword found grace in the wilderness;
*   when Israel sought for rest, the Lord appeared to him from afar.*
I have loved you with an everlasting love;
*   therefore I have continued my faithfulness to you.*
Again I will build you, and you shall be built, O virgin Israel!
Again you shall adorn yourself with timbrels,
*   and shall go forth in the dance of the merrymakers.*
Again you shall plant vineyards upon the mountains of Samaria;
*   the planters shall plant, and shall enjoy the fruit.*
For there shall be a day when watchmen will call
in the hill country of Ephraim:
*   'Arise, and let us go up to Zion, to the Lord our God.'"*

Am I too much of an optimist, Uncle? Comfort me again as you did when I was a child; reassure me there is reason to hope.

Blessings on you and on your brothers and sisters in exile,

from JEREMIAH

by the hand of Baruch

Sixth month
2nd year in the
governorship of Gedeliah

Dear Uncle,

Gedeliah has governed the remnant of Judah for well over a year, and we are every day more convinced of his worthiness. He has shown the attributes of a true leader: honesty, strength, idealism, kindness, and a sense of fairness. There is indeed a hopeful mood (as you remarked in your last letter) among those who live in Mizpah and the surrounding regions.

At Gedeliah's command the people planted winter and spring crops at the proper times, though many grumbled that we would not live long enough to harvest the fruits. They were wrong, of course; in fact we have gathered grain and fruits in great abundance.

One night not long ago I dreamed that the Lord again looked with favor on Judah and blessed all its inhabitants. The city-dwellers and the farmers and shepherds lived here together, and the weary people were replenished. Jerusalem became once again a place of righteousness and a holy site. Then I woke up and looked around to see where I was, and I was truly happy because I knew my dream was prophetic.

I do believe the days are coming when the Lord will gather the remnant of Israel from the farthest parts of the earth and make a new covenant with them. Man and beast will return to the land he promised to our forefathers; just as the Lord stood guard over our downfall, so he will stand over us during our restoration. The sorrow of the house of Israel and the house of Judah will be turned to joy.

Baruch has written down these words of repentance and hope which the Lord spoke to me after my dream:

> *"A voice is heard in Ramah, lamentation and bitter weeping.*
> *Rachel is weeping for her children;*
> > *she refuses to be comforted for her children, because they are not."*
> *Thus says the Lord: "Keep your voice from weeping,*
> > *and your eyes from tears;*
> > *for your work shall be rewarded, says the Lord,*
> > *and they shall come back from the land of the enemy.*
> *There is hope for your future, says the Lord,*
> > *and your children shall come back to their own country.*
> *I have heard Ephraim bemoaning, 'Thou hast chastened me,*
> > *and I was chastened, like an untrained calf;*
> > *bring me back that I may be restored, for thou art the Lord my God.*
> *For after I had turned away I repented;*
> > *and after I was instructed, I smote upon my thigh;*
> *I was ashamed, and I was confounded,*
> > *because I bore the disgrace of my youth.'*
> *Is Ephraim my dear son? Is he my darling child?*
> *For as often as I speak against him, I do remember him still.*
> *Therefore my heart yearns for him;*
> *I will surely have mercy on him," says the Lord.*

You see, Uncle, the Lord has again promised to forgive those who repent of their sins!

It is vital that the people know and understand what Yahweh expects of them, namely true repentance and amended lives. That is why the priests and prophets must study the word of the Lord and communicate it to the people; even more important, they must set an example before the people of how they should live their lives in accordance with the scriptures. Up until now, that has not happened very often, but I am convinced that the day will come.

Do you remember the proverb quoted so often by teachers of the law during the reign of King Jehoiakim? They would say:

"The fathers have eaten sour grapes,
and the children's teeth are set on edge."

It would be foolish to argue that the proverb is untrue; children have always suffered for the sins of their forebears. Yet I think it will happen some day that every one will suffer for his own sins; and each man who eats sour grapes, his own teeth will be set on edge. Likewise, each man will have the opportunity to repent of his own sins and be forgiven.

Am I getting too philosophical in my old age? Is my optimistic nature finally coming to the surface? The temple officials would never believe it if they heard me talking like this! You may show this letter to any of the exiled priests—I would be glad to know their reaction.

The boy Hanniel continues to sing and play beautiful music for Gedeliah and his courtiers. Baruch and I are often invited to hear the music and participate in the discussions which follow; it seems to me that the courtiers' disposition and judgment are much improved for having listened to psalms and gentle melodies.

Baruch has asked me to dictate more of these new thoughts to him so he can write them on a scroll. I will oblige him and ask him to write an extra copy to send to you. His hand will be sore, but his head and heart will be satisfied!

The grape harvest has been superb this year, so we shall have an abundance of good wine. I am putting aside several wineskins, in hopes that we may one day celebrate the return of the exiles from Babylon.

JEREMIAH
by Baruch

Ninth month
2nd year in the
governorship of Gedeliah

Dear Uncle,

Shaphan would be proud of his family, if he had lived to see this day. His grandson, the governor, leads the people boldly and decisively, yet without the haughtiness of the last two kings. He seems to remember that Yahweh is our one true king. Two of Shaphan's sons (Gedeliah's uncles) are acting as advisers to Gedeliah, and the governor's cousins are also leaders in the community, some by official appointment and some by the moral example they set.

It is fitting that Shaphan's family should play such a prominent role in bringing the people back to the Lord. Shaphan himself carried the newly discovered scroll, containing the book of the law, from the temple to the court of King Josiah, and he read it to the king. Now, thirty-seven years later, his children and grandchildren are still reading and taking to heart the words of the scroll. Sorcery, fortune-telling, and ritual sacrifice of sons and daughters have been strictly banned; the first fruits of our harvests are again offered at the altar of the Lord; and the people are honest and generous in their dealings with one another. Is it possible that the descendents of Abraham have finally cut off the foreskins of their hearts so that they might love the Lord with all their heart and with all their soul? Let us hope.

In recent days, I have been dictating to Baruch some poems about foreign nations. It is plain to me that Egypt will never be Judah's savior, no matter how formidable they look with their coats of mail and polished spears. Instead, they will expose their backsides to the enemy and run away, utterly terrified. The Lord of hosts has disheartened the warriors of Egypt, who knock their heads together, stumble, and fall. In vain they use medicines and seek the balm of Gilead, but they will not be healed.

As for Babylon, a powerful nation shall rise up out of the north and march against her. Shouting and firing many arrows, they will attack fiercely until her ramparts are crushed and she surrenders. Babylon, the hammer of the earth, will be pounded into the ground!

"In those days and in that time, says the Lord, the people of Israel and the people of Judah shall come together, weeping as they come; and they shall seek the Lord their God. They shall ask the way to Zion, with faces turned toward it, saying, 'Come, let us join ourselves to the Lord in an everlasting covenant which will never be forgotten.'"

Then all the exiles will return to Jerusalem and we will be united again as one family. May that day come quickly.

JEREMIAH by Baruch

First month
3rd year in the
governorship of Gedeliah

Dearest Uncle,

The Lord is good; he pours out blessings on his faithful servants. While others rejoice in their own wisdom, might, and riches, I glory in my understanding of the Lord. By his goodness, I am able to see certain things other people do not see. I know, for instance, that the Lord practices steadfast love for his people Israel, and that he delights in justice and righteousness on the earth more than burnt offerings.

Others will come to know these things, too, as his power and mercy and goodness are made manifest.

"Behold, the days are coming, says the Lord, when I will make a new covenant with the house of Israel and the house of Judah, not like the covenant which I made with their fathers when I took them by the hand to bring them out of the land of Egypt, my covenant which they broke, though I was their husband, says the Lord. But this is the covenant which I will make with the house of Israel after those days, says the Lord: I will put my law within them, and I will write it upon their hearts; and I will be their God, and they shall be my people. And no longer shall each man teach his neighbor and each his brother, saying 'Know the Lord,' for they shall all know me, from the least of them to the greatest, says the Lord; for I will forgive their iniquity, and I will remember their sin no more."

Yahweh is the faithful husband of Israel and we are his chosen. He is the potter who made us and the fountain of living waters who nourishes us. He will not abandon us, for we are his flock and the first fruits of his harvest.

Why all this poetry, you may ask? Why all this optimism? I feel new hope all around; I can see the seeds of restoration planted everywhere. The peoples' hearts are newly circumcised, prepared to know the Lord and accept his forgiveness. We are led by a wise governor who encourages worship of the Lord and observance of his laws. We have no need of false shepherds, the priests and prophets who feed only themselves, for the Lord himself has sought out and rescued his sheep, and he feeds them with good pasture.

It is not difficult for me to imagine a time when all the Hebrew people will return to the land with purified hearts. They will be ready to follow a wise king, to obey the laws written on their hearts, and to worship the Lord faithfully. Can you conceive of this? Has my imagination run wild? When I see the boy Hanniel studying the scriptures or playing music on the psaltery, I have confidence that these things will come to pass in his lifetime. I know he will see the return of the exiles, who will be ruled by a king from the house of David and led in worship by Levitical priests. The Lord will provide for the people shepherds who will feed them with knowledge and understanding.

In that day Jerusalem will be called the throne of the Lord, and all nations will come together to worship the Lord in Zion. The house of Israel and the house of Judah will once again be joined as a family in the land promised to their fathers.

We may not live to see that day, Uncle, but for me it is enough to know such things will come to pass. The Lord will do as he promised.

Baruch says I must include in this letter the prophecy which came to me last month, which he has already written in a scroll for his library. It concerns the same topics I have already written about today, but perhaps in a new light. The Lord said:

"I will gather the remnant of my flock out of all countries where I have driven them, and I will bring them back to their fold, and they shall be fruitful and multiply. I will set shepherds over them who will care for them, and they shall fear no more, nor be dismayed, neither shall any be missing, says the Lord.

"Behold, the days are coming, says the Lord, when I will raise up for David a righteous Branch, and he shall reign as king and deal wisely, and shall execute justice and righteousness in the land. In his days Judah will be saved, and Israel will dwell securely. And this is the name by which he will be called: 'The Lord is our righteousness.'"

If only we could be watching together as these things occur, I would live and die an exceedingly happy man. But, alas, the Lord has not granted us this blessing. We remain far apart, in different worlds, yet thinking alike and hoping for the same outcome.

The poems you sent are beautiful. I especially liked the ones expressing a longing for home, which for you has geographical meaning but for me is symbolic and spiritual. The home I seek is a land where the people know the Lord and live in right relationship with him, obedient to the laws he has written on the tablets of their hearts. May we someday meet in such a home!

With love,
JEREMIAH and Baruch

Fifth month
3rd year in the
governorship of Gedeliah

Dearest Uncle,

You will return to Jerusalem! The Lord has spoken, telling the exiles to mark and observe guideposts along the way, so that they might return on the same road by which they went to Babylon. The Lord has changed his mind and relented from the punishment he decreed.

Everything is turned upside-down. The man who was a great warrior cries in panic, holding his belly like a woman in labor. In that time of great distress, when every face turns pale and every mother loses hope for her sons, the Lord is creating something new; women protect their men. In desperation, wives and daughters find courage to strive vigorously, turning womanly weakness into strength.

Other things will change: The old covenant, written on stone tablets, was hidden in a box, sometimes lost, often ignored and forgotten. But the new covenant, etched deeply and painfully in the hearts of all the people, is different—it cannot be lost or forgotten because each person is to be given the knowledge and the intent to obey the Lord. A new relationship will be established between Israel and her husband Yahweh.

Those who survive the sword will be blessed. The destruction is complete, the punishment has been meted out, and at last the rebuilding and replanting can begin. The Lord loves Israel with an everlasting love; he continues in his faithfulness to her.

"Sing to the Lord, for he has triumphed gloriously;
the horse and his rider he has thrown into the sea."

Just as Miriam, after the exodus from Egypt, led the women in dancing with timbrels and singing this song, so we should celebrate the new exodus. Judah will return from Babylon and build houses and plant vineyards, and the watchmen in Ephraim will cry out, "Let Israel return to Zion, to the Lord our God."

Remember how the covenant with the Lord was renewed when King Josiah reinstituted the Passover observance, after four hundred years of neglect? In like manner, the Lord will establish a new covenant with this nation after they return to him. It is pleasing, Uncle, to be allowed to preach good news of hope and encouragement after so many years of finding fault. Perhaps the Lord is rewarding his unworthy servant for long hours of prayer and study. No! As soon as I start giving credit to myself, things go wrong. It is better not even to think such thoughts!

JEREMIAH by Baruch

Fourth month
4th year in the
governorship of Gedeliah

My dear Uncle,

What you recently told me about your fellow exiles in Babylon confirms and strengthens my belief that you, the exiles, are the faithful remnant of the Hebrew people. You have more faith, greater determination to obey the laws of Moses, and a truer understanding of what the Lord requires of his people than those who were left behind.

I wish the people here understood as well as you that there is only one Lord, and him only must we love with our whole heart and soul and might. Even now, many people in Judah cannot bring themselves to abandon Baal, Merodach, Nabu, and the other so-called gods who exist only as impotent objects of wood and stone. You are right in concluding that Yahweh is the only God, the one who created the earth and who rules over all things.

When you deny the existence of Merodach and refuse to bow down to his image, I know you risk your lives. It is distressing to hear of the young men in your community who endure torture and cruelty at the hands of your captors. Those who suffer in this way have obeyed Yahweh's call to be a light to the nations, carrying his righteousness to the ends of the earth. It is true (as the prophets have said) that Israel is to be a servant of the Lord in all the world.

The conditions of our lives here continue to improve. We consume good wine and good food, we celebrate marriages and births, and for the most part, we enjoy amicable relations with the Chaldean soldiers who patrol the land. Sometimes I think the day of restoration has come, as told me by the Lord:

In this place of which you say, "It is a waste without man or beast," in the cities of Judah and the streets of Jerusalem that are desolate, without man or inhabitant or beast, there shall be heard again the voice of mirth and the voice of gladness, the voice of the bridegroom and the voice of the bride, the voices of those who sing, as they bring thank offerings to the house of the Lord: "Give thanks to the Lord of hosts, for the Lord is good, for his steadfast love endures for ever!" For I will restore the fortunes of the land as at first, says the Lord.

Thus says the Lord of hosts: In this place which is waste, without man or beast, and in all of its cities, there shall again be habitations of shepherds resting their flocks. In the cities of the hill country, in the cities of the Shephelah, and in the cities of the Negeb, in the land of Benjamin, the places about Jerusalem, and in the cities of Judah, flocks shall again pass under the hands of the one who counts them, says the Lord.

But still I have doubts. I am not certain we have suffered sufficiently for our sins and the sins of our fathers. Have we become truly righteous before the Lord? Are we ready to accept the love of our divine shepherd who will count each one of us as we pass under his hands? I cannot banish the doubts and apprehensions from my head, much as I have tried.

To dwell again on the good news, our harvests have been so plentiful for the last two years that we laid aside surplus grain in storage houses. Our leaders are practicing wiser and more far-sighted policies than I have ever seen in Israel. The governor has appointed his old uncle Elasah to oversee agricultural affairs, and he has found intelligent, industrious men to advise him in other areas as well. Gedeliah is not afraid to surround himself with competent advisors, even though they might gain power and prestige at his expense.

We began harvesting the barley crop a month ago, and it was so bounteous that even old men like me were put to work. Many years had passed since I tried to swing a sickle, and before long my back was aching. A young woman noticed my distress and pulled me aside to help her bind up the sheaves. Even this was exhausting work, and consequently I slept quite well during the harvest time.

When all was gathered in, we presented the usual thank offering to the Lord, but that was not the end of our celebration. The young men shouted and sang, and the women prepared a sumptuous feast of roasted lamb with chick-peas and barley bread. We sat around the fire for hours, eating and drinking and listening to Hanniel play soft melodies on the harp. Weary and sunburned as we were from weeks of exertion in the fields, we felt a surge of energy and exuberance at having completed the harvest.

And yet, all is not well. Within a few hours of the harvest feast, a brawl erupted on the edge of town. Some of the young men had too much to drink and, according to reports, one of them was not able to get his way with a woman he desired. He picked a fight with another young hothead who had ridiculed him, and soon all their friends joined the fray.

The Babylonian soldiers charged with keeping the peace tried to break up the fight. They succeeded, but not before a couple of them were injured rather badly. As a consequence, all the people in Mizpah have been put under curfew, so they are allowed to leave their houses only on business during the day and not at all during the night.

Why do some people insist on causing trouble when things are going well? Instead of appreciating the good which prevails, they extend their personal problems to a wider sphere, causing unnecessary misery for all.

As you might guess from this letter, my mood has been fluctuating over the last few months and even during the last week. I have no clear vision of the future for the people of Judah. At times I am affected deeply by their righteousness and goodness, and at other times, I despair at their depravity. It is no easy thing to be a prophet when human behavior is so inconsistent!

Best wishes from JEREMIAH
with Baruch

Diary entry:

The Chaldean soldiers have always treated me well, ever since they first came to Jerusalem. Yesterday they waved me through the line of sentries posted around Mizpah and allowed me to leave the city. I had no particular destination in mind but hoped to roam the hills for a few hours in solitude.

After wandering a good distance from the city, I followed a little brook up the side of a rocky hill. As I passed by a patch of scrubby bushes, I heard what sounded like moaning, so I turned aside from the path to investigate. Behind the bushes was a small grotto or indentation in the rock, where lay a feverish, bleary-eyed man, partially covered with cut branches. Only a hard-hearted person would have left him there without stopping, so I asked if I could do anything for him.

"Help me," he said in a husky, weak voice.

"Tell me what is the matter," I answered.

"My back aches and my loins are burning."

There was something familiar about this man, but I did not immediately recognize him. His disease, however, was easily discernable from the symptoms; I noticed open sores on his skin and a cloudy film over his eyes, as well as his flushed face. The man was suffering from the deadly affliction by which Yahweh punishes those who visit the cult prostitutes.

"Can you not help me?" he pleaded.

"Here is some cool water," I said, holding out my water pouch.

He snatched it from my hands and began pouring water in the direction of his face. A little went into his mouth, but most ran down his neck onto the dusty ground. At this point, I recognized him to be Zaccai, Mara's cowardly husband, and I felt nauseated with revulsion. Immediately I began to upbraid him for deserting his wife and children and leaving them to die in Jerusalem.

"Mara is dead then?" He began to sob, "May the Lord have mercy upon me."

"It is better than you deserve," I answered, with scorn in my voice.

"It is true. I deserve death, but I am afraid to die. I beg you to save my life. I will give you everything I own."

I could not imagine that this man had anything of value to give away, and furthermore there was nothing I could do to save him. But I stayed with him. During the next few hours, he drifted between uneasy sleep and semi-conscious frenzy, at times babbling about his hunger and thirst and his fear of being caught by the Babylonians. I soaked a piece of bread in water and placed it on his tongue, but he could not swallow.

After several hours, Zaccai's face turned pale. He suddenly sat up and looked directly at me (although I am not sure if he ever knew who I was), and he said in a clear voice, "I have been running for four years and I can run no more." Then he fell back and died. This miserable man was much to be pitied.

I could not, by myself, bury Zaccai in the hard, dry earth, but upon my return to Mizpah I told some young men where they could find the body (if the vultures did not find it first). Seeing Zaccai put thoughts of Mara into my head, and thinking about her fate put me in a gloomy mood. In that mood I might have remained for days had not young Hanniel come knocking on my door.

He had no particular reason for coming, except to talk with me about his ideas, just as I used to do with my Uncle Shallum. Hanniel has always loved to hear and play music, and lately he has wanted to discuss those aspects he finds most interesting and attractive. He is fascinated by songs he heard in the camp of the Chaldean soldiers, which are quite different from our songs, he tells me. Some of his analysis was beyond my comprehension, having to do with sequences of tones, but I listened attentively and understood the gist of what he was saying. It is refreshing to see such enthusiasm for good and wholesome things, especially in a young person.

It gives me hope for the future to see a thoughtful youth like Hanniel, who frequently laughs at himself and yet takes other people seriously. The boy has a good head and a good heart, which is not surprising considering the family in which he grew up. His father, his uncles, and his grandfather are righteous men who have served the Lord well. They have also been loyal friends who rescued me from many dangerous situations. Ahikam and his brothers saved me from execution more than once. Even old Shaphan protected me on several occasions from angry temple officials. Furthermore, the women of the family welcomed me into their houses, fed me, and tended to my needs when others in Jerusalem were embarrassed or afraid to be seen with me. I owe much to this family, and I love the boy Hanniel for their sake and for his own.

As I reflect on past experiences, I often wonder how much longer the Lord will command me to prophesy. Whenever I start to think my work is appreciated and I feel pride in my own talents and accomplishments, the Lord quickly blesses me with failure, which jolts me back to reality. It is not, after all, my innate abilities on which success depends, but my trust in the Lord. If I rely utterly on him for strength and inspiration, I am swept along on a huge wave of succor and support, giving me confidence that I can accomplish whatever it is he wants me to do. Yet I often forget this and fall back into worry and uneasiness.

And thus I waver between self-doubt and confidence in the Lord; I must remember that his love surrounds me and, if I acquiesce, this love will swallow up all irritations and disappointments.

Twelfth month
4th year in the
governorship of Gedeliah

Dear Uncle Shallum,

Baruch has again annoyed me by comparing me to Moses. He said the Lord raised me up as a prophet like Moses and put words in my mouth and I spoke them. Well, perhaps I did, but so did many other prophets!

Moses claimed he could not speak well and consequently the Lord gave him Aaron as a mouthpiece. When the Lord called me, I was too young to speak in public, but that excuse did not satisfy the Lord Yahweh. He touched my mouth, gave me the words, and sent me out on my own. No one else ever spoke for me, as Aaron did for Moses. It is true Baruch has read my dictations in public a few times, and I admit he sometimes transcribes my words more eloquently than I speak them, but he has never been a mouthpiece for me.

I do not recall hearing that Moses was harassed and mocked by the Israelites, as I have been. In his infancy he was cast into the Nile River to prevent his being killed by the Egyptians, but did his own people ever try to kill him? Did they throw him in a pit?

Furthermore, I ask if Moses wept bitterly at the iniquity and shame of Jerusalem? No! He never saw Jerusalem; he died outside the promised land, spared the vision of devastation I have witnessed. Moses did not see the house of the Lord become a heap of ruins, hissed at by those who pass by.

Surely he did not experience doubts about his call to be a prophet, as I have done. In all ways, Moses was a much better man than I, and Baruch insults him by making the comparison.

I am sorry, Uncle, for this ranting. You see my mood is affected by concern that the Jews here are once again forgetting the Lord and falling back into their habitual pattern of self-reliance and self-congratulation. Pray for us.

JEREMIAH by Baruch

Blood

Fourth month
5th year in the
governorship of Gedeliah

Dear Uncle,

It looks as if this will be another good year for the farmers. The winter crop was excellent, and the spring plantings appear robust in the fields. The favor of the Lord is surely with us, for we have enjoyed four successive years of abundance.

Not everything looks as auspicious as that, however. There have been rumblings lately about a plot against Gedeliah instigated by the Ammonites. Instead of attacking directly, the Ammonite king has evidently recruited some of our Hebrew men to cause trouble.

One of our most reliable military leaders, Johanan, came to Mizpah to warn Gedeliah. He claims that Ishmael, a member of the royal family and former officer of the king, is plotting to kill him. The governor does not seem overly concerned; after all, Ishmael has been his friend for a long time. I cautioned Gedeliah to take seriously any reported threats against his life, even from the most unlikely conspirator.

But there are happier topics to write about. Time passes quickly, and my young friend Hanniel has become a man. His voice is already deeper than mine and his beard is beginning to sprout. He loves to sit with me and discuss the law and the prophets. I experienced the oddest feeling the other day when Hanniel asked me the same question I had asked you some thirty years before! I will try to recreate my recent conversation with Hanniel; then you must tell me whether you remember a similar discussion we had long ago.

"Why does Yahweh allow bad men to become wealthy and powerful and influential?" he asked.

"That's a difficult question," I said.

"Yes, but it happens all the time. If the Lord loves us, it seems he would protect us from those men who trample others to get more for themselves."

"Perhaps he expects us to protect ourselves."

"But not everyone can protect himself. Remember the woman from the east side of town whose house and land were taken away by her rich neighbor?"

"I think it may be the responsibility of her other neighbors to seek justice for her. The Lord inspires each of us with a sense of fairness and gives us opportunities to oppose evil where we see it. Can we blame the Lord if we fail to act according to our best judgment? Are we not able to recognize wrongs and uphold what is good and right?"

Do you recognize my answer, Uncle? It is essentially the same one you gave me many years ago. I told Hanniel that even my wise old Uncle Shallum had not been able to give a complete answer to such a difficult question. It is likely you have gained insight in the years since then; tell me any new ideas you have on this subject.

Thank you for the many answers you have given me through the years. Sometimes when I think about a hard question, your voice rings in my ears and then I am able to give a thoughtful answer.

JEREMIAH with Baruch

Sixth month
5th year in the
governorship of Gedeliah

Dear Uncle,

Something terrible is waiting just outside the door. When we open the door, it will devour us, along with our wives, our children, our flocks, and our fields. I long to escape the evil news that is coming; I am weary of grieving for Israel.

Finally I understand: they are unable to change their evil behavior. Winnowing the people will not separate the good from the bad, for the evil is ingrained in all. The Lord hates their sin and will do battle with it until it is finally killed. He is close at hand, judging and chastising even those who love him. In carrying out his purpose, his rule is firm.

The law says that the man who reviles the Lord and despises his word shall be entirely cut off. Rebellion against the sovereignty of Yahweh cannot be forgiven. When a person rejects the one who forgives, he thereby spurns the possibility of forgiveness.

While the people of Israel were still in Egypt, the Canaanites defiled the land with their perversions. The Lord punished their iniquity, and the land vomited out its inhabitants. Now the apostasy of Israel is so great and so intractable that the Lord can stomach her no longer. His judgment will come swiftly and the land will vomit out its inhabitants once again.

It is beyond my understanding why we sin and suffer. Nevertheless, I have no doubt that the Lord has led me with his strong hand, during sad times as well as joyful times. Though I have accomplished only a little in my life, I am comforted by the thought that he does not need me to carry out his work. He can bring good out of bad and life out of death to accomplish his purpose. Now I wait.

May your faith be strengthened as mine has been,
JEREMIAH and Baruch

Seventh month
5th year in the governorship
of Gedeliah

Dear Uncle,

What is happening in Mizpah? There is blood everywhere: on the walls, on the ceiling, in the doorway, on every object in my house. My sleeping pallet sits in a pool of blood. My clothes are soaked, and I can taste blood in my mouth and feel it oozing on my skin.

Where does it come from? I don't know, but I think it must be a fountain or a spring. Even the one who follows me around has blood dripping from his eyes. Have you seen a man (if he is indeed a man) with red eyes and gleaming white hair? He has followed me for many years but never told me his name. I think he is the source of the blood, because it seems to flow from his eyes.

I don't know where Baruch has gone. I have called out to him again and again, but he won't come. Another person, who is very kind, offered to write a letter for me. I am sorry that the words are written in blood, but I hope you can read them anyway.

When I find a messenger, I will send this letter right away because I know you want to hear the news from Mizpah. If you see Baruch, please send him to me.

JEREMIAH
by the hand of Jeshua

First month
1st year after the
governorship of Gedeliah

Dear Uncle,

After the last letter I wrote, you would be justified in questioning the health of my body and mind. I was in a horrible state from having witnessed events which I could not accept as true. I still wish we could go back in time and erase those events, which seem to me more like a nightmare than reality.

Baruch found me soon after I had sent the last letter. He thought it would be wise for us to go into hiding, considering what had just occurred. I was in no condition to oppose his wishes, so after nightfall we made our way to a small cave on the outskirts of town. We were not the only ones who thought to hide there—in fact it was already full of refugees. We survived a few days in the cave with very little food and barely enough room to sit down.

When conditions had become nearly intolerable, we heard the sound of horses and raucous laughter outside the cave. Our "deliverers" had arrived. Ishmael's men ordered us to come out and return to our houses and stay there until further orders were given. We obeyed, of course.

Now, dear Uncle, I must tell you about the events which led up to this unfortunate day. It is difficult to speak of these things, but you and the other exiles must be informed of what has happened here.

Remember I told you earlier of rumors that Ishmael, in league with the Ammonite king, was plotting to kill the governor. Gedeliah would not believe the rumors; to show his trust in Ishmael, he invited him and ten of his men to dine with him. While they were eating, the contemptible traitor Ishmael stood up and thrust his sword through Gedeliah, inflicting a mortal wound. Then he and his men killed all the Jews who lived with Gedeliah in his house and the Chaldean soldiers who were there on assignment.

As if that wasn't enough, the next day, before anyone knew Gedeliah had been murdered, eighty Samaritan pilgrims arrived in Mizpah on their way to Jerusalem. They carried grain offerings and incense which they hoped to present at the temple of the Lord, not realizing, poor souls, they would find only rubble at the site.

Ishmael went out from the city to meet them, uttering false greetings and bidding the pilgrims come visit the governor Gedeliah. As soon as the pilgrims entered Mizpah, Ishmael and his men turned on them and slaughtered them, all but a few who pleaded for mercy and offered bribes. Then he dumped the bodies into a huge cistern which became a pool of blood. Imagine what it was like to find the bodies of those pilgrims and then to discover the scene of carnage in the governor's house. Soon after that, I wrote you a letter by the hand of Jeshua, which I fear must have bewildered you.

The people are thoroughly frightened. For the time being, we live under house arrest, afraid to venture outside into streets patrolled by brutal killers. We do not know what to expect next, but we need no further proof of Ishmael's evil intent.

Gedeliah was a fine man and a good leader. The community here was thriving and growing each day in righteousness and prosperity. Now we have nothing. What is happening? Where are we going?

JEREMIAH
with Baruch

*Third month
1st year after the
governorship of Gedeliah*

Dear Uncle,

Much has happened since I last wrote to you. The people in Mizpah became confused and timid when their leader Gedeliah was murdered. Ishmael, the killer, seized power immediately and was able to exact obedience through force and intimidation. All the residents of Mizpah were his captives.

For the second time in my life, I was driven like an animal to a holding area outside the city, along with all the other people in Mizpah, to prepare for a long march. This time we were tied together with heavy ropes which our captors knotted tightly around our waists. Ishmael then commanded that we start walking toward the Ammonite country.

I understood perfectly well why King Nebuchadnezzar took so many of our people into exile in Babylon; he deported those exiles to make use of their skills and labor in bolstering the Babylonian economy and also to curtail rebelliousness in Judah. But it makes no sense at all that one of our own Hebrew men, a member of the royal family no less, should take the remainder of his people over to the Ammonites. It was a sad procession that left Mizpah.

Ishmael had not reckoned on any resistance, so people were allowed to loosen their fetters when we stopped for the night. We were asleep by the great pool in Gibeon when someone started shouting at the edge of the camp. It was too dark to see what was going on, but we heard unmistakable sounds of fighting. Then a horseman rode through camp and told us to scatter and find cover away from the fighting.

When morning came, we learned that Johanan and all the forces with him had followed us from Mizpah and attacked Ishmael during the night. Ishmael and his men managed to escape, but the people nevertheless rejoiced to be freed from their latest captivity. Baruch and I urged Johanan to take the people back to Mizpah, but Johanan had other ideas.

He led the people south, past the ruins of Jerusalem, to our present camping ground in Geruth Chinham, near Bethlehem. Johanan is afraid to face the Chaldeans because the governor they appointed was slain by one of our people. I tried to convince Johanan that the Babylonian leaders are reasonable men and that we have nothing to fear. But he has it in his head that we should go to Egypt for protection. Since when have the Egyptians protected us from any military conquest?

I fear the days ahead will bring only frustration and hardship. Now that Gedeliah is gone, there is no leader who stands out above the others for his wisdom, honesty, and faithfulness to Yahweh. I pray that someone will emerge to lead us, but I have little hope. Will our troubles never end?

JEREMIAH
by Baruch

Fourth month
1st year after the
governorship of Gedeliah

Dearest Uncle,

My work will soon be finished, in one way or another. These people will finally succeed at what they have been striving to do for such a long time: to silence the word of the Lord in the land of Israel. They will surely suffer the consequences and be removed once and for all from the land promised to their fathers Abraham and Isaac and Jacob.

For years I have tried to warn them, but they were deaf to my words. When trouble came, they blamed me for their misfortunes. They ridiculed me, beat me, and tried to kill me. Now, you may ask, what more can they do?

They want to take me away to Egypt, to an unknown fate, far away from the land of my fathers. Why should they carry away an old man? Who am I to excite their fears to such a high pitch that they will not leave me to die in peace? Why am I not left behind to prophesy to an empty land, where the stones listen with greater attentiveness than the people?

The events of the last month have left me disheartened. After Ishmael and his band of rowdies slew the governor Gedeliah, the leaders of the people came and asked me to pray to the Lord, that he might show us what we should do next and where we should go. Johanan and the other leaders swore they would obey the voice of the Lord.

I prayed to the Lord for ten days. His answer, when it came, was not ambiguous:

If you will remain in this land, then I will build you up and not pull you down; I will plant you, and not pluck you up; for I repent of the evil which I did to you. Do not fear the king of Babylon, of whom you are afraid; do not fear him, says the Lord, for I am with you, to save you and to deliver you from his hand. I will grant you mercy, that he may have mercy on you and let you remain in your own land.

If you set your faces to enter Egypt and go to live there, then the sword which you fear shall overtake you there in the land of Egypt; and the famine of which you are afraid shall follow hard after you to Egypt; and there you shall die.

Do you think, Uncle, that the leaders of the people kept the promise they made to obey the voice of the Lord? Certainly not! They said I was telling a lie. They accused Baruch of turning me against them so that I would deliver them into the hand of the Chaldeans to be killed or carried into exile. Can you think of a sillier accusation? How could anyone regard Baruch—dear, faithful, honest Baruch—as a traitor?

Nevertheless, the leaders are planning to take to Egypt all the remnant of Judah, men, women and children, even those members of the royal family who were not taken into exile. They will force me to go with them, and Baruch as well.

In all likelihood, this will be my last letter to you. Take care of yourself, knowing that Yahweh will one day restore the fortunes of his faithful people and return them to their homeland. Pray, Uncle, that the Lord will have mercy on us.

Now I will close with a psalm you taught me:

Let this be recorded for a generation to come,
so that a people yet unborn may praise the Lord:
that he looked down from his holy height,
from heaven the Lord looked at the earth,
to hear the groans of the prisoners,
to set free those who were doomed to die;
that men may declare in Zion the name of the Lord,
and in Jerusalem his praise,
when peoples gather together, and kingdoms,
to worship the Lord.

With all our love,
JEREMIAH and BARUCH

Tahpanhes, Egypt

Dear friend Shallum,

This is the first letter that I alone have written to you. It might never reach you, and perhaps it would be best if you did not hear the news it contains. I am sending the letter with Egyptian traders whose caravan will pass through Judah on the way to Damascus, and I am hoping they can find someone to carry it to you in Babylon. It seems rather unlikely, but I feel I must make an attempt to communicate with you.

After Gedeliah was murdered, you remember, Jeremiah said plainly that the remnant of the Jewish people should stay in Judah. But the leaders ignored his counsel; they forced everyone to go with them to Egypt. We have been living in Tahpanhes for a number of years, although I have lost track of the date by our usual reckoning. The time spent here has been turbulent.

At Jeremiah's request, I kept a history of our stay in Egypt from the moment we arrived until now. I will copy some parts of the history for you, to illustrate how Jeremiah persisted in speaking the word of the Lord, even after he was forcibly transported to a foreign country.

"In the first month after we arrived, Jeremiah picked up large stones and buried them in the mortar at the entrance to Pharaoh's palace. Then he spoke the word of the Lord to the men of Judah, saying that Nebuchadnezzar king of Babylon would erect his royal residence on the site above these stones. This would happen after he conquered Egypt, striking with his sword, spreading pestilence, and taking many captives. He would shatter the obelisks in Heliopolis and burn down the temples of the Egyptian gods, decontaminating the land as a shepherd would decontaminate his vermin-infested coat.

Johanan, our leader, was disturbed to hear these words from Jeremiah. He spoke with Pharaoh's officials, trying to convince them to silence the prophet or put him under house arrest. The Egyptians merely scoffed at what they regard as 'Hebrew foolishness,' and so Jeremiah was allowed to continue speaking among the people.

The Egyptians decided it would be wise to separate us, the Jewish population, into four smaller groups, to prevent our becoming too powerful. One contingent was sent to live in Migdol, one to Memphis, one to the land of Pathros, and one (including Jeremiah) told to remain in Tahpanhes. The groups were allowed to communicate freely with each other, but not to stay long away from their assigned cities.

In the year after the division into four groups, Jeremiah preached to the Jews living in Egypt. He reminded them how the people in Judah had offended the Lord Yahweh by burning incense to other gods, even though the prophets warned them not to do this abominable thing. Therefore the Lord brought terrible misfortune to the people of Jerusalem and all the cities of Judah.

Jeremiah told the leaders they had committed a great sin by removing all the Hebrew people from Judah, leaving no remnant of Jews in the land promised to our fathers. Moreover, they forgot the consequences of their earlier infidelity, and they burned incense to other gods in Egypt. Never did they repent or submit to the Lord or acknowledge the laws which he gave to our forefathers.

As a consequence, the Lord decreed that the Jews who came to live in Egypt would be killed, all of them, even while they were dishonored and cursed and reviled. The Hebrew people in Egypt shall be punished as Jerusalem was punished, and only a few shall escape or return to the land of Judah."

Dear Shallum, as I copy out this history for you, I can hardly believe the audacity of the people in their response to Jeremiah. They defied the Lord, even as they insulted and scorned his faithful prophet.

"The people said they would not listen to Jeremiah. They vowed to continue the idol worship they had practiced in Jerusalem. Not only would they pour out libations to the queen of heaven; now the women would bake cakes with her image on them! This they did with the approval of their pathetic husbands.

These statements infuriated Jeremiah. He said to all the people, and especially to those women, that they should confirm their vows to worship the queen of heaven and should live up to those vows. He said the Lord Yahweh therefore had sworn that his name would never again be invoked by the Jews living in Egypt. The Lord said he would bring them misfortune rather than blessing. As a sign, he would allow the king of Egypt, Pharaoh Hophra, to be captured by his enemies, just as King Zedekiah of Judah was captured by Nebuchadnezzar."

Of all the words I heard Jeremiah speak during his long career, this utterance was most hideous: that the name of the Lord would never again be invoked by these men. They were doomed to worship false gods for the rest of their lives and forbidden to turn again to the one true God. Can you imagine anything so horrible? Yet it seems a just outcome. These people persisted for such a long time in their waywardness that the Lord finally allowed them to have their own way.

I will summarize for you the rest of the history. Jeremiah condemned the rulers and people of many foreign nations for their pride and contempt of the Lord, including the Philistines, Moabites, Ammonites, and Edomites. He finally spoke against Nebuchadnezzar king of Babylon and the Chaldeans, saying they would be conquered and put to shame for the evil they committed against Israel, atrocities the Lord had not commanded them to do. Then Jeremiah prophesied against Egypt and put his life at risk, for the Egyptians did not wish to hear themselves criticized, even by a "crazy man." As a consequence, they offered encouragement to Jeremiah's enemies, who now felt they had license to stir up a riot the next time Jeremiah preached to the Jews in Tahpanhes, and so those enemies achieved the result they had long sought.

Dear friend, if you receive this letter, know that I am weeping with you in my heart as you read it. The people were swept into such a frenzy that they picked up stones and began throwing them at Jeremiah. He was not deterred but kept preaching the word of the Lord. They picked up larger and larger stones and hurled them with increasing force as he spoke. Several stones found their mark and brought forth blood from his head and neck, but even as he fell to the ground he continued to prophesy. When it was over, he was covered with blood, his white hair and beard turned scarlet. I went to him and fell over his body, weeping and mixing my tears with his blood. Finally, my friends pulled me away and carried the body to a safe place. We buried Jeremiah, prophet of the Lord, in Egypt; but I promise you, if I am ever allowed to leave, I will carry his bones back to Jerusalem, to the home he loved and the people he served.

Jeremiah said that the Jewish exiles in Babylon would one day return to Jerusalem. When it happens, they will find scrolls containing Jeremiah's sermons and writings, and they will know that he was a prophet of the Lord. He will continue to speak to them long after his death, and a few will listen.

Blessings to you, my dear Shallum,
from Baruch

Scripture Citations
(Revised Standard Version)

CHRONOLOGY (Dates B.C.E.)

640   630   620   610   600   590   580   570

Historical Events:
- 622 Torah scrolls found in temple; reforms begin
- 612 Babylonians conquer Nineveh
- 605 Babylonians take northern Israel
- 597 Babylonians take Jerusalem; First exile of Jews to Babylon
- 588 Jerusalem rebels; siege begins
- 586 Judah falls to Babylonians; Temple destroyed; Second exile of Jews to Babylon

Rulers of Judah:
- 640 King Josiah — 609
- 609 King Jehoiakim 598
- 598 Prince Jeconiah
- 597 King Zedekiah 586
- 586–582 Governor Gedeliah

Life of Jeremiah (Approximate Dates):
- 626 Jeremiah called as prophet
- 609 Temple sermon
- 605 Scroll cut up
- 597 Letter to exiles
- 594 Yoke on neck
- 588 Slaves freed; Jeremiah leaves Jerusalem
- 587 Buys field; dropped in well
- 582 Taken to Egypt
- 570 Prophecy from Egypt